Learning
Team
Skills

Learning
Team
Skills

ARTHUR H. BELL, PH.D.

DAYLE M. SMITH, PH.D.

School of Business and Management
University of San Francisco

NETEFFECT SERIES

Prentice
Hall

Upper Saddle River, New Jersey
Columbus, Ohio

Library of Congress Cataloging-in-Publication Data

Bell, Arthur H. (Arthur Henry).
    Learning team skills / Arthur H. Bell, Dayle M. Smith.
       p.   cm.
    Includes bibliographical references and index.
    ISBN 0-13-033674-2
    1. Teams in the workplace. I. Smith, Dayle M. II. Title.
   HD66 .B443 2003
   658.4'02—dc21   2001059180

Vice President and Publisher: Jeffery W. Johnston
Senior Acquisitions Editor: Sande Johnson
Assistant Editor: Cecilia Johnson
Production Editor: JoEllen Gohr
Production Coordination: BookMasters, Inc.
Design Coordinator: Diane C. Lorenzo
Cover Designer: Ceri Fitzgerald
Cover art: Corbis Stock Market
Production Manager: Pamela D. Bennett
Director of Marketing: Ann Castel Davis
Director of Advertising: Kevin Flanagan
Marketing Manager: Christina Quadhamer

This book was set in Goudy by BookMasters, Inc. It was printed and bound by Hamilton Printing. The cover was printed by The Lehigh Press, Inc.

Pearson Education Ltd., *London*
Pearson Education Australia Pty. Limited, *Sydney*
Pearson Education Singapore Pte. Ltd.
Pearson Education North Asia Ltd., *Hong Kong*
Pearson Education Canada, Ltd., *Toronto*
Pearson Educación de Mexico, S.A. de C.V.
Pearson Education—Japan, *Tokyo*
Pearson Education Malaysia Pte. Ltd.
Pearson Education, *Upper Saddle River, New Jersey*

10   9 8 7

ISBN 0-13-033674-2

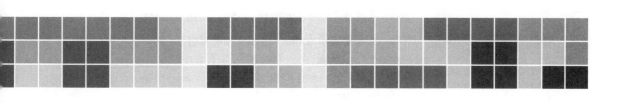

Contents

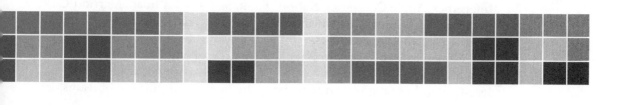

Preface

As with other books in this series, we intend this discussion of teams to be more of a conversation than a lecture. At frequent points throughout these chapters, you will have a chance to "talk back" in the Your Turn exercises. We hope you will use these opportunities to write down your experiences, attitudes, objections, insights, and feedback. In this way you will participate with us in learning about teams and their importance in organizational life.

You can talk back in a more immediate way by e-mailing us with your questions, comments, thoughts, and reflections about the contents of this book. Please contact us at bell@usfca.edu—and plan to receive a response within 48 hours or sooner.

ACKNOWLEDGMENTS

We are grateful for the decades of scholarship by thousands of professors, researchers, and social scientists that allow us to speak more confidently now about the proven advantages of teams in organizations, the skills of team leaders and members, and the ways team problems can be overcome. Our current academic colleagues at the School of Business and Management, University of San Francisco and past academic colleagues at Harvard University, University of Southern California, and Georgetown University have been generous over the years in sharing their insights about the nature and workings of teams. Equally generous with their ideas and experiences have been the many executives and managers we have met in our consulting work for teams in dozens of companies and organizations, including Price-Waterhouse Coopers, TRW, Lockheed Martin, IBM, Citicorp, PaineWebber, the U.S. State Department, China Resources, Charles Schwab, Sun Microsystems, Cost Plus World Market, the Colonial Williamburg Foundation, American Stores, Deutsche Telekom, New York Life, the U.S. Coast Guard,

Infogenics, Apple Computer, Nations Bank, Santa Fe Railroad, Marriott Corporation, the Central Intelligence Agency, the Private Industry Council, Bain & Co., and Quaker Oats.

We dedicate this work to Gary Williams, Dean of the School of Business and Management, University of San Francisco—a friend, leader, and colleague who has taught us much about the power and purpose of teams.

Art Bell
Dayle Smith

Belvedere, California

OTHER BOOKS IN THIS SERIES BY BELL/SMITH

Learning Team Skills
Motivating Yourself for Achievement
Managing Your Time
Interviewing for Success
Building Your Network

Why Teams?

GOALS

- Understand advantages of the team approach to work.
- Grasp importance of "buy-in" for team effectiveness.
- Relate team concepts to your own work opportunities and challenges.

Although analogies tend to hide as much as they reveal, let's begin our conversation about teams by considering sports teams. Perhaps we can learn basic lessons from basketball, football, baseball, and other team sports that can enlighten and inform our approach to work teams.

What's your ticket? Basketball? On the court, five players form a team. One person, of course, could dribble the ball downcourt and shoot (making basketball a one-on-one sport similar to tennis singles), but the sport has evolved as a team endeavor for at least five reasons:

1. A team offers the possibility of more talent on the floor. All parts of the game move more quickly due to the specialized skills of individual players and the mutual cooperation of team members.

Imagine the limitations of one player compared to the team. That person would have to do it all, including jumping, shooting, rebounding, playing defense, and so forth. At least two disadvantages of this approach come to mind. First, the person probably cannot be equally good at each of those sports skills. A great rebounder, for example, is not often a great ball-handler or dribbler. Second, the player who tries to do it all quickly becomes exhausted.

Let's translate this basketball analogy into the practical world of business and other organizations. In business and school endeavors, you require a broad range of talent to understand problems, recognize opportunities, and carry on the many processes necessary to meet the organization's goals. Even the smallest company needs someone adept at financial management, someone attuned to personnel recruitment and development, someone to oversee operations, someone who is good with the public and press, and yes, someone to sweep the floors at night. This team understands the importance of allowing each member to do his or her job. Team members are careful not to trespass unnecessarily onto one another's job responsibilities. In short, they trust one another to carry out each of their specialized tasks. The company as a whole works well because each member of the team performs well.

INSIGHT 1	The team approach brings together the specialized skills of many individuals to resolve problems, seize opportunities, and meet organizational goals.

Your Turn

Call to mind a team on which you served in business or school. List the specialized strengths of each of the team members. Was the team missing any particular skills it needed to reach its goals? If so, how did the team make up for this skill deficit?

2. Each player can count on backup in case of a stumble, a bad game, or an injury.

A team provides an insurance policy of sorts for unexpected interruptions and disabilities. Even when one of the team's stars is unavailable for play, the concerted efforts of other team members can often make up the difference and achieve success.

In the same way, a team in a business or academic setting ensures that important goals can be met regardless of the ups and downs of individual team members. Too much is at stake in such environments to risk failure over one member's sudden ill health, family emergency, job transfer, or other unexpected circumstance. The Broadway slogan for this ongoing effort continues to be, "The show must go on." The cast—or team—pulls together to fulfill its mission even if key members are missing in action.

| Teams provide a backup system that ensures continuity and mission fulfill-ment even if particular team members are unable to perform. | **INSIGHT 2** |

| | **Your Turn** |

Think about a time when a team on which you served was "left in the lurch" by the sudden absence of one of the key members of the team. Did your team survive this change? If so, how did your team compensate for the missing member? What was the ultimate result?

3. Individual eccentricities are tempered by the team for the good of the game.

In basketball, some players love to shoot the ball. Even when they miss repeatedly, they try and try again. If their failure to consistently make baskets begins to harm the team's efforts and success, team members take it upon themselves to change the "ball-hog's" behavior. When the team refuses to pass the ball to the ball-hog, the message comes through loud and clear: Quit shooting all the time and become more of a team player. In this way, individual idiosyncrasies are suppressed for the good of the team effort.

Similarly, on business and school teams, the wild ideas of some team members get tested by the judgment and experience of the rest of the team. If the team as a whole rejects the wild ideas of one member, those ideas usually fade away and play no role in the eventual report, project, or other activity developed by the team. This self-censoring function of teams is a valuable aid to upper management. Without the idea filters naturally provided by teams, upper management could easily face a plethora of documents, all written by individuals, and all expressing highly individual ideas about company problems and opportunities. It would then be the difficult task of upper management to sift through the set of often bizarre ideas in search of a few that made sense. Teams take much of this burden from upper management by squelching unworkable ideas from the outset.

| Peer pressure on teams operates to enforce common sense judgments and ideas. Extreme or impractical ideas are usually rejected by the team before such ideas find their place in the work output of the team. | **INSIGHT 3** |

Your Turn

Think about a time when one of your team members expressed an idea that was judged to be "crazy" or "way off track" by the rest of the team. How did other team members let this person know that the idea did not meet the approval of the team? How did the person react? What was the ultimate result for the person and the team?

---

4. Motivation increases as team members take pride in one another and try not to let each other down.

When members of a basketball team win their league championship, they do not come to the microphone to speak about "motivation from my million dollar salary" or "special treatment I was given by the coach." Instead, they almost always talk about the inspiration they received from their teammates; the effort all members gave so as not to let each other down; and the powerful influence each member felt by seeing other team members working so hard for victory.

That same kind of team motivation occurs in business and school environments. When a meeting is called for 9:00 A.M., you try to be on time, not merely because your boss expects promptness, but because you respect the time of your fellow team members. You do not want them sitting around waiting for you to arrive. When an approaching deadline requires that the team work late, you do your part in seeing the project through to completion. You are willing to go the extra mile not only because you want the project to be successful, but because you do not want to let your teammates down.

This is not to say that we automatically become close friends with all team members we serve with over the course of a business or academic career. Some team members don't earn our respect and it is hard to feel much obligation, responsibility, or liking for them. But other team members—perhaps the majority we encounter—are hard-working, well-intentioned coworkers with whom we feel bonds of camaraderie. In these cases, a significant factor in our motivation to do a good job and see the project through to success stems directly from our feelings toward other team members. Esprit d'corps on a team, in fact, can be one of the most powerful motivators in professional life.

INSIGHT 4

Teams whose members respect and like one another gain the advantage of motivation internal to the team. Members of the team want to perform not only for external rewards, but for the internal rewards of partnership, mutual respect, and friendship engendered within the team.

Recall a team made up of people you liked and admired. How did these positive feelings toward other team members influence your performance on that team? Would you have performed differently if you had little liking or admiration for your fellow team members?

5. The task of beating the opponent requires the combined talents of five players.

Finally, teams are required in sports because opponents are strong and shrewd. In other words, external challenges have much to do with the necessity for forming teams. In the case of basketball, it would be folly for a single player to go up against an opposing team of five players. Teams form in response to the challenges they face.

Let's take business examples of this same principle. If the "opponent" to a new product is millions of consumers who don't know about the product, a company wisely assembles a marketing team to take on this significant challenge. If a competitor comes out with a similar product to your own but priced considerably less, your company will probably act quickly to put together a response team made up of representatives from marketing, research and development, accounting, operations, and other specialities to determine how this challenge can be met and overcome.

Powerful challenges must be met by powerful responses. Such power often comes in the form of a talented, motivated team. **INSIGHT 5**

Remember a time when your company or school organization faced a significant challenge or problem and, in response, formed a team on which you served. In what ways was the membership of the team determined by the nature of the challenge or problem? In your opinion, were members well-chosen for the responsibilities they had to perform? How successfully was the challenge or problem met by the team?

TEAMS AND BUY-IN

In the best of all worlds, companies would be made up of individuals, work groups, departments, and divisions all equally committed to reaching common company goals. In such a world, the head of finance would not mind giving up 50 percent of his department's budget if that sacrifice would help the Marketing Department do a better job for the company.

Anyone who has worked even a few days in an organization of any size quickly realizes that politics play a major role in determining the behavior of individuals and groups. The head of finance, for example, probably had to battle long and hard against other department heads for his share of the company budget. He will battle even harder to keep other departments from taking his budgeted money or otherwise intruding on his turf. In many companies, work groups and departments seem to be more concerned with their own growth and financial support than with the overall welfare of the company. This competition for resources pits all divisions in the company against one another in an ongoing political wrangle that consumes enormous energy and attention.

In such a political minefield, the steps and missteps of one division alone may be doomed to disaster. "That's a report from marketing," the head of accounting may bluster. "They've skewed everything to support their own needs." The head of marketing may be just as suspicious of any data or other information sent forward exclusively from accounting. How does business get done in such a charged environment where the left hand doesn't trust what the right hand is doing?

The simple answer is teams. By assembling representatives from the various political entities within the company, upper management ensures that the work product of the team will be generally acceptable to all company members. "After all," the head of marketing explains, "we had one of our people on that team. Our interests were represented." Other department or division heads feel similarly. In short, the buy-in assured by the membership of the team extends to its work product. A report from the team, for example, will be greeted with much more credibility by the company as a whole simply because that document arose from the combined efforts of somewhat opposed interests.

INSIGHT 6	Even though teams and teamwork may be more cumbersome and time-consuming than individual action, the team approach may nevertheless be justified, in large part, for the buy-in it facilitates in politically charged organizational environments.

Your Turn	

Think about a time when you served on a team made up of individuals representing different and perhaps opposed interests within the company or organization. Was it difficult for the team to make decisions? If so, why? Did the team complete its work? If so, was that work widely accepted by the company or organization?

TEAMS AND CENSORSHIP, PRO AND CON

As discussed earlier, a team provides an early-warning system and an effective suppression mechanism for member ideas judged by the team to be impractical or outlandish. Filtering out such ideas at an early stage saves money and organizational energy. Imagine the damage a wrong-headed idea could do if allowed to proceed forward in the development of a project or other company activity.

On the other hand, teams must exercise caution that they do not become guilty of what Harvard professor Irving Janis has called Group-Think. This phenomenon occurs when a group refuses to hear ideas or information in conflict with the majority opinion. The group may put too much stock in the strength-in-unity notion, to the point that all dissent is ridiculed or angrily dismissed. Influential group members may urge other team members to adhere to the party line for the sake of group harmony.

Perhaps the classic case study of GroupThink occurred at Morton Thiokol Corporation in the days just prior to the Challenger disaster. Although one engineer, Roger Beaujolais, raised serious concerns about the safety of "O"-ring functions at low temperatures, his dissent was discounted by Morton Thiokol project managers and ignored by NASA administrators. These managers and administrators felt pressure from their superiors and from the press, including Dan Rather's reporting on the nightly news, to launch the often-delayed shuttle. Safety concerns aroused by the "O"-ring matter did not fit in with NASA's overarching agenda. The team in this case squelched dissenting information that could have saved the mission as well as the lives of the astronauts involved.

GroupThink can be prevented in teams by getting all members to agree to several procedural guidelines:

- Rules of order (such as Robert's Rules of Order) should not be used to silence dissenting opinions.
- Pressure for consensus should not be applied in such a way as to prevent the expression of minority perspectives.
- Each team member should be a critical evaluator of team processes. In doing so, team members must call attention to symptoms of Group-Think that occur during team discussion.
- The team leader must not impose a preordained perspective or foregone conclusion on group members.
- The group must welcome outside information and opinion, especially when such input disagrees with the dominant direction of team discussion.

INSIGHT 7	In suppressing worthless and impractical ideas, the team must be careful not also to suppress valuable dissent.

Your Turn
Bring to mind a time when you or another team member disagreed strongly with the direction of discussion and decision making taken by your team. How was that disagreement presented? How did other team members respond? What finally happened?

TEAMS AND CROSS-TRAINING

An additional defense of teams arises from the need for cross-training in organizations of all kinds. When specialists gather as members of a team, a certain amount of cross-fertilization takes place. Like actors in a play, each team member learns at least a portion of the "lines" of other team members. For example, an advertising specialist on the team shares her approach to product marketing with the human resources (HR) representative. Even though the HR representative does not then become an instant expert on advertising, he or she nevertheless has important insights into the art of advertising and can add to discussion and decision making on the topic. If the advertising team member had to miss a meeting, others on the team would be able to carry on, thanks to their cross-training.

Companies and other organizations maximize the contributions of their employees by such cross-training. Especially in economically stressed times, companies may not have the luxury of hiring specialists as needed for every project underway in the company. Upper managers must rely on employees to use not only their first areas of expertise, but also their background knowledge in secondary areas (achieved through cross-training) to keep projects on target and on time.

Cross-training within teams can be facilitated in at least two ways:

■ Take regular cross-training breaks from usual team activities. For example, you can devote an hour every few meetings exclusively for sharing core aspects of each member's expertise and techniques. Rather than overloading any one meeting with too much cross-training data, one or two team members can share their perspectives and knowledge at each cross-training occasion. Put in common terms, a cross-training session can be labeled, "How to Think Like a . . . (marketing, finance, operations, etc.)."

■ The team can invite outside expertise to visit team meetings with the goal of sharing techniques, skills, and concepts as an upgrade to the existing knowledge and skill base of team members.

Cross-training makes each team member more valuable to the team and ensures against knowledge and skill gaps during the life of the team.	**INSIGHT 8**

Your Turn
If you have received valuable cross-training as a part of your membership on a team, tell about that cross-training and how you used it. If you have not received cross-training in this way, write briefly about the kind of cross-training you would like to receive and how it could help you contribute to the team.

TEAMS AND FOLLOW-UP RESPONSIBILITIES

Like most assemblies of individuals, a team has a life span ranging from a matter of days to several years. No matter how long the team survives, someone must remain active and available as its spokesman, interpreter, and perhaps defender. Here's an example of follow-up responsibilities after a retailing team finished its work. Someone had to

■ present team findings to several levels of management
■ draw together team documents, data, and meeting notes
■ answer questions about what the team decided, meant, suspected, and recommended
■ meet with other teams who wanted to learn from the success of the previous team or continue its work in some way

Although these duties often fall to the team leader, they can be assumed by other team members. A high-performing team can distribute these follow-up responsibilities among its members partly to lighten the load on the team leader and partly to prevent team history from being rewritten in the retelling by just one member.

The work of a team is not over after the team's last meeting. Many important follow-up responsibilities can be distributed among team members.	**INSIGHT 9**

Recall the aftermath activities of a team on which you served. What kinds of things happened after the team's last meeting? Who took responsibility for those tasks and opportunities? Did the person(s) do a good job? If not, what improvements in follow-up responsibilities can you suggest?

TEAMS AND THE SOCIAL ASPECT OF ENTERPRISE

Finally, teams have the advantage of being more enjoyable than most work accomplished all alone. Here's the opinion of one manager in the computer industry after a 6-month period of service on a 6-member team within her company.

> We met at least once a week. Even though we didn't know one another before our first meeting, we quickly gelled into a comfortable and stimulating work group. I looked forward to seeing my teammates each week for at least four reasons. First, I wanted to find out how their individual portion of our work was going. Second, I needed perceptive people to hear about the work I had accomplished and give me meaningful feedback. Third, we all needed other people with whom to share our joys and frustrations about the project. Finally, we just got along as people. Although we didn't spend a lot of time on social talk, there was the inevitable chat about kids, pets, hobbies, life stresses, good restaurants, interesting movies, and so forth. For all those reasons, I found team membership much more energizing and fulfilling than simply laboring away by myself in my cube.

INSIGHT 10   Most people have a natural tendency to seek out the company of others. This tendency can help to make teamwork more motivating and fulfilling than the same work undertaken alone.

Compare a time when you accomplished a project or task by yourself with a time when you accomplished a similar project or task as a member of a team. Which form of work was most fulfilling to you? Which was most efficient? Why?

Summing Up

Teams offer many advantages as an organized way to accomplish tasks. First, work teams have all the positive qualities of sports teams in extending available expertise, coordinating knowledge and resources, and utilizing internal modes of motivation. Second, teams provide a means of achieving buy-in in politically charged work environments, where opposing interests may resist accepting the work product of any one constituency in the oganization. Third, teams act to censor worthless ideas before they negatively influence the development of decisions and projects. Fourth, teams encourage cross-training, with resulting advantages to the company in case particular specialists are unavailable. Fifth, teams provide more people to handle follow-up responsibilities than in work accomplished by a single individual. Finally, teams are often fun work experiences. Such enjoyment and satisfaction promotes employee loyalty, motivation, and commitment.

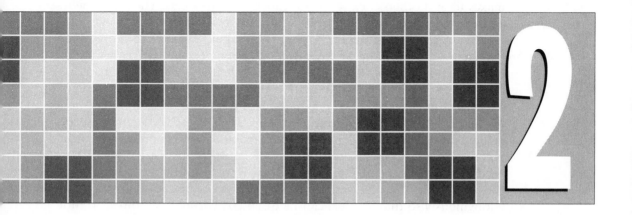

Assessing Your Team Experience and Insights

GOALS

- Assess characteristics of effective team membership and leadership.
- Discover evaluation instruments that can lead to productive discussion of team issues.
- Develop personal priorities for improvement in team skills.

The poet Robert Burns wished that "the gift God would give us/To see ourselves as others see us." His sentiment echoes that of Socrates: "Know thyself." In both cases we are being counseled to delve beneath the surface layers of self-congratulation and image enhancement to learn what really makes us and others "tick" as team leaders and members. The instruments and exercises contained in this chapter can prove helpful in moving beyond subjective assessment ("What I think about myself") to more objective analysis ("How I appear to others"). Like the personality test contained in *Developing Leadership Abilities* (Bell/Smith, Prentice Hall, 2002), Chapter 2, these instruments provide information that may indicate major tendencies, strengths, and weaknesses in our individual portfolios of team skills. These test indications are best used as a starting place for self-reflection and development rather than as a judgment of any kind on one's present or future potential as a team member or leader. The results of these exercises are best used as the focus for in-depth discussion by all team members, including the team leader. In some cases, you may want to complete the instruments anonymously so that answers can be discussed without any threat to individuals on the team.

Exercise 1	What Do You Expect of a Team Leader?

Directions: Put the following qualities associated with team leadership in order of your perception of importance, 1 through 11, with 1 being highest. Then compare your ranking with that of 7 years of surveys recently published in *Best Practices*[1] magazine.

I believe a team leader should be (in order of importance):

Dependable_____

Straightforward_____

Broad-minded_____

Intelligent_____

Forward-looking_____

Honest_____

Imaginative_____

Courageous_____

Fair-minded_____

Inspiring_____

Competent_____

---

[1] "Establishing the Credibility Factor," *Best Practices*, January 1999, p. 121.

Here are the percentages of thousands of survey respondents who ranked the importance of these qualities:

Honest 87%
Competent 74%
Forward-looking 67%
Inspiring 61%
Intelligent 46%
Fair-minded 42%
Broad-minded 38%
Courageous 35%
Straightforward 33%
Imaginative 32%
Dependable 31%

We each have different expectations of a team leader. The same leader can fulfill the expectations of some members of the team while disappointing other members. A team can usefully discuss its expectations of leadership and communicate those expectations to the team leader.	**INSIGHT 11**

Your Turn

Choose two or more qualities that you ranked significantly higher than the survey respondents. Explain why you believe the qualities you selected are of special importance for an effective team leader.

When the Team Makes a Mistake   Exercise 2

Directions: Write down three mistakes for which a team could easily be forgiven or that could be used without penalty as learning experiences, such as not keeping detailed minutes of their team meetings. Once you have completed your three items, try to find them on the list of actual team mistakes gathered from managers and supervisors by researcher Deborah Harrington-Mackin; all mistakes in her list were judged as forgivable by these business professionals.

(continued)

Exercise 2   When the Team Makes a Mistake (continued)

I believe teams can be easily pardoned for making the following mistakes:

1.

2.

3.

The following is Deborah Harrington-Mackin's[2] list of forgivable team mistakes. A team's mistakes can be accepted and forgiven by management if:

- the mistake doesn't have significant negative impact upon the company
- it is a first-time mistake, not part of a pattern
- team members were working outside the team's usual area of responsibility
- the team member was following explicit instructions or proper procedures
- the team member was working with shared equipment that was not always available
- the team learns from the mistake and is able to say how it will be avoided in the future
- the mistake occurred within the scope of the team's authority in pursuit of the team's goals
- the team was really trying to do things right
- the team's actions were consistent with the policies and rules of the company
- incorrect information was given to the team
- the team was taking initiative and reasonable risks
- procedures weren't clearly defined by management
- different skill and ability levels of team members caused erratic results
- there were extenuating circumstances
- the situation was outside the team member's control
- the error was not caused by negligence or lack of action
- there were unavoidable time constraints
- there was poor training

[2] Harrington-Mackin, Deborah. *Keeping the Team Going.* New York: American Management Association, 1996, p. 15.

Knowing that your team can and will make pardonable mistakes frees each member of the team to take risks, explore options, and "push the envelope" of imagination.	**INSIGHT 12**

Your Turn

Recall a past job, perhaps a summer job, in which your boss at the time was critical of each mistake you made as a new employee. (If you have not had this work experience, recall a person in your life who has been too critical of your missteps.) How did you respond to the threat of criticism hanging over your head? Did it help your work performance in any way? Did it hinder that performance in any way?

Who Pulls Your Strings as a Team Member? — Exercise 3

Directions: Each member of the team, including the team leader, should complete the following assessment, then compare and discuss results with one another. From its discussion of the results of this instrument, the team can accurately appraise the various types and degrees of influence perceived by the team.

For each worker category, circle the number that best represents your estimate of influence this worker category has on your performance as a team member:

Category	Very High	High	Moderately High	Some	Little	Very Low
CEO/President	6	5	4	3	2	1
Top managers	6	5	4	3	2	1
Mid-level managers	6	5	4	3	2	1
Team leader	6	5	4	3	2	1
Team members	6	5	4	3	2	1
Subordinates	6	5	4	3	2	1

Team members often seem as if they are acting in response to an unseen boss. Learning who that perceived boss is can help team members distinguish their real priorities from imagined ones.	**INSIGHT 13**

Your Turn

Think about a time when you had to guess what your boss was thinking about you, your job, and company operations. (This approach to management is called MBM—Management by Mystery.) How did this uncertainty affect your work performance and attitude toward your job?

Exercise 4   Does the Team Control Its Own Destiny?

Directions: Circle the "a" or "b" option you most agree with for each pair of questions. Then transfer your answers to the interpretive scoresheet. Your cumulative totals under the respective columns will indicate the degree to which you believe the team to be in control of its own destiny or controlled by forces external to the team.

1. a. Team members must often deal with issues they do not understand and cannot control.
   b. Team members understand most issues they deal with and have substantial control in their decisions regarding those issues.

2. a. The value of the team's work is usually determined by the hard work and insights of the team members themselves.
   b. The value of the team's work usually depends on how well others in the organization do their work.

3. a. A good team leader is born, not made.
   b. Depending on the situation, any member of a good team can perform well in the role of team leader.

4. a. Teams fail most often due to internal strife and lack of focus.
   b. Teams fail most often because they lack organizational power and support.

5. a. The amount of support given to a team in an organization depends primarily on the intelligence and fairness of top management.
   b. The amount of support given to a team in an organization depends primarily on how well the team makes its case for deserving support.

6. a. The success of a team is often due as much to good fortune or luck as to good work.
   b. The success of a team is almost always due to the quality of its work.

7. a. Teams that make careful plans for their activities usually succeed.
   b. Teams do better to remain flexible because changes in the marketplace and in organizational priorities usually can't be anticipated.

| **Does the Team Control Its Own Destiny? (continued)** | **Exercise 4** |

8. a. Being a valuable team member depends most of all on one's previous level of power in the organization.
   b. Being a valuable team member depends most of all on one's ability to listen well and respond intelligently.

9. a. The work of competent teams is usually rewarded in the organization.
   b. Organizational rewards go most often to teams with the right contacts inside and outside the organization.

10. a. Team skills can be learned by almost all employees.
    b. A significant percentage of employees could never learn to be good team members.

Scoresheet

Perception of External Control Over Team   Perception of Internal Control Over Team

1a _____	1b _____
2b _____	2a _____
3a _____	3b _____
4b _____	4a _____
5a _____	5b _____
6a _____	6b _____
7b _____	7a _____
8a _____	8b _____
9b _____	9a _____
10b _____	10a _____
Totals _____	_____

| The issue of control is crucial for any team. Team members who feel that they have little to say or do about their own destiny may show signs of discouragement and lack of initiative in working on team projects. | **INSIGHT 14** |

| | **Your Turn** |

Recall a time in your work or academic life when you had little control over the activities and duties expected of you—you had to do them but had little choice over what, where, or when. How did this lack of control affect your performance and attitude?

Exercise 5   How Effective Is the Team Leader?

Directions: Using the scoresheet provided, circle the number that comes closest to your opinion for each statement. A total of all your circled scores will provide a single number measurement of the leader's effectiveness, at least in your opinion. The lower the final total score, the more effective the team leader is in your view.

1. The team leader supports my efforts on the team.
2. The team leader usually goes along with decisions of the team.
3. The team leader accepts differences of opinion among team members.
4. The team leader makes good use of time spent in team meetings.
5. The team leader is a good listener to problems I face as a team member.
6. The team leader makes sure that I am fairly rewarded for my work on the team.
7. The team leader helps the team resolve its internal conflicts.
8. The team leader helps team members develop and improve.
9. The team leader leaves many important decisions up to the team.
10. The team leader treats all team members fairly.

Scoresheet

	Strongly Agree	Agree	Slightly Agree	Slightly Disagree	Disagree	Strongly Disagree
1.	1	2	3	4	5	6
2.	1	2	3	4	5	6
3.	1	2	3	4	5	6
4.	1	2	3	4	5	6
5.	1	2	3	4	5	6
6.	1	2	3	4	5	6
7.	1	2	3	4	5	6
8.	1	2	3	4	5	6
9.	1	2	3	4	5	6
10.	1	2	3	4	5	6
Totals	____	____	____	____	____	____

Cumulative total of all scores: ____

Team members should take this assessment anonymously and present scoresheets to the team leader for review and discussion. Once these perceptions are known to the team leader, goals can be set for both the team leader and team members to achieve more effective relations with leadership.

INSIGHT 15

Although team relationships depend on more than the leader's action, this key figure has much to do with the way team members think about themselves, their work, and the team itself. By understanding their feelings about the team leader, team members can make the most of the leader's strengths and find ways to address his or her weaknesses.

Your Turn

Think about a time when you worked for or served under a leader you did not like or respect. Did you communicate your feelings to this person in any way? How did your feelings toward the leader influence your work performance and personal satisfaction in the position?

Assessing My Participation in Team Meetings   Exercise 6

Directions: Each team member and the team leader should fill out the following assessment as soon as possible after a team meeting. Results should then be discussed openly as a direct means of improving team relationships and interaction.

1. Where I sat during the meeting. Sketch your seating position in relation to other team members.

2. How this seating position influenced my participation.

3. Types of participation during the team meeting. Place numbers in each blank according to the following scale: 1—Agree; 2—Not sure; 3—Disagree.
   _____ I spoke up to initiate new ideas.
   _____ I spoke up to disagree with other speakers.
   _____ I spoke up to agree with other speakers
   _____ I spoke up to offer additional information.
   _____ I spoke up with questions.
   _____ I spoke up to clarify points for others.
   _____ I spoke up to summarize points for others.
   _____ I spoke up in a humorous way related to the point at hand.
   _____ I spoke up in a humorous way unrelated to the point at hand.
   _____ I did not speak up.
   _____ Other forms of participation: (specify)

(continued)

Exercise 6	**Assessing My Participation in Team Meetings (continued)**

4. My attitudes toward participation. Place numbers in each blank according to the following scale: 1—Agree; 2—Not sure; 3—Disagree.

____ I felt I expressed myself clearly and persuasively.

____ I felt I expressed myself clearly but not persuasively.

____ I felt that I did not express myself clearly or persuasively.

____ I felt that the team usually let me have my say.

____ I felt that I was usually cut off by other team members before having my say.

____ I felt that I spoke up too often.

____ I felt that I wanted to speak up more often, but did not.

____ I felt that I spoke up too little.

____ I felt that I communicated an impatient attitude toward the meeting.

____ I felt that I communicated a discouraged attitude toward the meeting.

____ I felt that I communicated an upbeat, energetic attitude toward the meeting.

INSIGHT 16	The usual forum for team gatherings is in a meeting. A team member's physical position in the meeting room and ways of participating in the meeting itself can tell much about the team member's relationship to the rest of the team and that member's contributions to the work of the team.

Your Turn
Call to mind the last meeting you attended. In your view, was it a good, bad, or indifferent meeting? Write out how you reached your judgment about the meeting. What aspects of the meeting were important to you in arriving at your judgment?

Summing Up

Talking about what's right and what's wrong with a team can often be difficult for team members and the team leader. A variety of exercises offer insightful questions that should be answered by the entire team. These answers can form the basis of a productive discussion of team policies, procedures, processes, and problems.

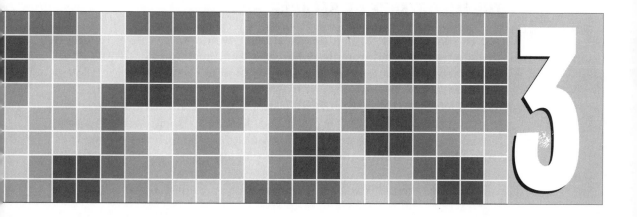

Building a Balanced Team

GOALS

- Grasp the importance of balance among member types for a productive team.

- Learn the main components that work together to create team balance.

- Become acquainted with techniques for building and restoring team balance.

Do you remember the process most of us used in elementary school to select team members for playground sports? Two captains (often self-selected!) would take turns choosing players for their teams. If you were one of the last chosen, that process was often painful indeed. Just as often, the teams ended up with various forms of imbalance: the boys against the girls, one set of friends against another set of friends, and so forth.

Teams in companies and other organizations cannot afford imbalance based on bias, whim, or accident. Just as a major league sports team endeavors to fill each position with talent, so a company tries to build teams whose members have complementary skills and backgrounds.

THE IMPORTANCE OF BALANCE

You can imagine the difficulties a company would encounter if it turned an important marketing project over to a team made up exclusively of accountants. It is likely that every aspect of the project would be judged solely and narrowly by its cost. Just as disastrous would be the assignment of financial reform in the company to a team made up of advertising specialists. In these examples, the presence of an accountant or an advertising person on the team is not in question; both would probably play a valuable role. Only when the team is composed of one employee type do difficulties often arise.

Consider the many ways in which teams can achieve balance:

- by mixing team member personality types
- by mixing team members according to their expertise and experience
- by mixing team members according to their place in the organization's hierarchy
- by mixing employee ethnicities
- by mixing employee genders

In all cases, the purpose for such balancing is not political correctness but improved bottom-line results for the team. The balance sought for any specific team depends on the purpose or project at hand, the audience to whom the team will report, and the company culture itself. Therefore, no single formula can be given as an ideal recipe for the balanced team. Instead, this chapter points out options and advantages you may want to consider when building a team in your organization. We focus especially on the advantages of gender balance.

INSIGHT 17	Balance in the membership of a team gives the company the differing perspectives of several stakeholders. Variety of opinion makes for more complete discussion of issues and, eventually, better decision making.

Your Turn

If you believe you have served or now serve on a balanced team, jot down any advantages and disadvantages that came as a result of the team's diverse membership. If you have never served on a balanced team, think about a recent team experience. Describe the kinds of members that, if added, would have made your team more balanced.

CAUSES OF TEAM IMBALANCE

Although imbalanced teams arise for many reasons, four causes in particular appear to account for most imbalanced teams.

The team as the boss's clones. In many companies, bosses have such high opinions of themselves that they appoint team members strictly in their image. For many years, IBM struggled with this cloning phenomenon on its sales teams: All IBM sales representatives seemed to look, act, dress, and think in remarkably similar ways. Certainly, in the last decade, IBM has acted aggressively to achieve the advantages of diversity in its workforce and on its key teams.

The team as the usual players. The old business adage asserts that "20 percent of the employees do 80 percent of the work." Unfortunately, some companies take this folk wisdom so literally that they keep appointing only that 20 percent to company teams.

The same people seem to appear on major company teams year after year and, with no surprise, probably tend to make the same kinds of decisions (or mistakes) year after year.

The team as those most suited for the task. At first glance, this form of imbalance makes a certain amount of sense. For example, it would seem logical to give a research project to a company team made up of researchers, but an imbalance of any one employee type yields less than satisfactory results. The team could no doubt profit from the addition of a member from the finance group or marketing department. These members could help researchers see the "big picture" and avoid intellectually interesting but impractical decisions.

The team as one personality type. Some companies make the right move in balancing teams with employees of differing backgrounds, only to make the greater mistake of choosing members all of whom share the same personality profile. For example, imagine a team composed entirely of obsessive planners, each with their Palm Pilot crammed with dates, deadlines, and schedules. Their team project will almost certainly be delivered on time, but may be sorely lacking in creativity and fresh thinking. The same general point could be made for teams composed entirely of any of the other personality types discussed later in this chapter.

Uniformity in membership usually has little advantage to a team. Diverse personality types, expertise, experience, and other differences among members tend to enrich discussion and improve decision making.	**INSIGHT 18**

Your Turn

As a speculative exercise, think of some work- or school-related project that might well be accomplished by a team. Describe the characteristics of at least five members—your "dream team"—that you would assemble to serve on that team. Explain why you aimed at the balance you describe.

HOW AND WHEN TO PLAN FOR BALANCE

Like balancing a car tire, the balancing of a team is better undertaken before the journey begins, so to speak, than when you're already on the road. Once you have formed a team, there is great stigma attached to removing a team member for any reason. Therefore, make it your priority to choose team members wisely from the outset of a project. Many managers follow these approximate steps in shaping the membership of a team:

- Write down the specific goals you want to achieve through your team.
- List any constraints (such as personnel availability, budget factors, and company policies or procedures) that will limit your choice of team members.
- Describe skill or expertise categories (not specific people) that should be represented on the team.
- Describe personality types that will help the team function optimally.
- Nominate in writing several people, if possible, for each of the skill or expertise categories you have described. For each person on this list, write down an educated guess about his or her basic personality type.
- Select team members who fulfill the desired skill or expertise categories and provide a useful distribution of personality types in relation to your project goals.
- Inform these individuals in a motivating, morale-building way of their membership on the team. (You will want to make yourself available for individual conferences to deal with questions and concerns.)
- Plan carefully for an inspiriting first meeting of the team, at which basic information regarding goals, team leadership, available resources, milestones, deliverables, and evaluation measures are thoroughly discussed.

INSIGHT 19   Productive teams rarely happen by chance. The effort a manager puts into the selection of team members is repaid many times over by the team's cooperative proceedings and significant achievements.

Think about a time when you found yourself as a member of a team that was apparently assembled without forethought or planning. If the efforts of the team were not successful, explain reasons for this failure. If the efforts of the team were successful, explain any adjustments team members had to make to deal with the lack of planning in the forming of the team.

THE LIMITS OF PERSONALITY TESTS

Team members typically exhibit personality tendencies that can be placed at some point on four continua:

Member —— Self
Thinker —— Empathizer
Planner —— Juggler
Closer —— Researcher

Experts in personality testing caution against an overly simplistic interpretation of personality types or test results. Human beings are complex bundles of intellectual and emotional potential that resist any single label. As you may have guessed, stress levels and other life circumstances can dramatically influence one's dominant personality type. For example, a Juggler (someone who likes to have many balls in the air at once and live in the excitement of the moment) may, during times of stress, revert to a rigid Planner mentality, complete with a daily "to-do" list of things to accomplish. A Thinker, who usually values proof, rationality, and logic can, under the impact of stress, exhibit qualities of the Empathizer.

The key to evaluating the personalities of team members (or potential team members) lies in knowing your people as thoroughly as possible. If you have not worked with them personally, talk at length with their previous supervisors and coworkers to learn about their work habits, attitudes, needs, and career goals.

Personality tests are only a starting point for the accurate description of your own personality or someone else's. Use the results of such tests carefully and in combination with other evidence to develop an appropriate balance of personality types on a team.

INSIGHT 20

Do you believe that your personality changes in significant ways during times of stress? If so, what are those changes?

MAKING THE MOST OF GENDER BALANCE

In the 1990s, several influential books (including Deborah Tannen's *You Just Don't Understand* and *Talking from 9 to 5*,[1] and Kathleen Reardon's *They Don't Get It, Do They?*[2]) have argued that many aspects of women's verbal and non-verbal communication in business are distinctly different from those of men. Moreover, these authors assert, women's communication habits sometimes put them at a disadvantage for leadership roles, team participation, promotion, recognition, and full participation in decision making in corporate life.

For our purposes, the goal of every team leader and member should be to understand possible communication differences between genders so that the contributions of both genders can be maximized. In some descriptions of team processes, the topic of women's modes of communication has been reduced to a latter-day version of Henry Higgins' complaint of Eliza Doolittle in *My Fair Lady*: "If only a woman could be more like a man!" Teams and team leaders who have a similar attitude toward women members are missing the unique contributions women bring to the team table. As Tannen, Reardon, and others point out, women's communication habits in business exist for reasons. To understand those reasons is to put ourselves as team members and leaders in a better position to make the most of the communication patterns of both men and women. In short, women and men who serve together on teams must learn to listen to themselves and to one another, then to make adjustments in communication styles to achieve fairness, make the best use of team resources, and successfully execute the organization's mission.

Let it be said at the outset that the following observations are by no means applicable to all women in business environments. No researcher of women's communication behaviors has claimed universality for the results of quite limited studies. In the words of Deborah Tannen,

> I do not imply that there is anything inherently male or female about particular ways of talking, nor to claim that every individual man or woman adheres to the pattern, but rather to observe that a larger percentage of

---

[1] Tannen, Deborah. *You Just Don't Understand.* 2d ed. New York: Quill, 2001; *Talking from 9 to 5.* 2d ed. New York: Quill, 2001.
[2] Reardon, Kathleen. *They Don't Get It, Do They?* New York: Little, Brown, 1995.

women or men as a group talk in a particular way, or individual women and men are more likely to talk one way or the other.[3]

Tannen's research, joined by dozens of supportive studies, makes the point that women do appear to communicate differently than men in work environments, including teams. Most often women have been judged negatively for this difference, and they have been instructed (often by women) to "talk the talk" (i.e., the male talk) if they want to rise to positions of power in companies and be taken seriously in teams. This effort to recreate women's communication patterns in men's images ignores the very real contributions women bring to the team through their ways of communicating. As a counterbalance, then, to the pervasive argument that women should learn to speak more like men, we offer brief interpretations of 20 gender communication patterns. These interpretations are intended to point out the value of women's communication patterns *as they are* without repair or alteration for modern teams.

Gender-based patterns of communication, whether those of men or women, can be useful in a variety of business circumstances and are equally of value.	**INSIGHT 21**

Your Turn

Give your own impressions of ways in which communication may differ somewhat depending on the gender of the communicator.

CHARACTERISTICS OF MEN'S AND WOMEN'S COMMUNICATION HABITS

1. Men are less likely to ask for information or directions in a public situation that would reveal their lack of knowledge.

Man: I don't need to stop at the gas station for directions. I can find the right street.

Woman: Why not stop and ask? It will save us time.

---

[3] Tannen, Deborah. *Talking from 9 to 5*, p. xxi.

The willingness of women to seek help in such situations can prove useful to what Peter Senge has called "the learning organization,"[4] including its learning teams. The reluctance, out of pride or embarrassment, of independent men on a team to seek assistance is counterproductive. The language habits of women in this case can be extended throughout the team as a way of encouraging openness to new information, reliance on team members as resources, and a constant readiness to ask questions and learn.

2. Women perceive the question, "What would you like to do?" as an invitation for discussion and negotiation. Men perceive the same question as the stimulus to a direct answer.

> Woman: We have to arrange a holiday party. What would you like to do? [She is expecting conversation about past holiday parties, anecdotes, personal memories, and possibility thinking.]

> Man: We have to arrange a holiday party. What would you like to do? [He is expecting places and times to be named.]

Women's willingness to delay decision making pending a multidimensional review of background information and influences is sometimes portrayed as a deficit, especially for would-be leaders of teams. However, that same communication tendency can be valued as an antidote to a team's tendency to rush to judgment or to ignore relevant input. On modern teams, leaders are cast less and less in the role of quick-draw decision maker and more in the role of seer, with wisdom and patience implied. The gender communication approach of women in this case fits well with the requirements of team leadership, where instant answers and quick decisions are often impossible or foolhardy.

3. Women misunderstand men's ultimatums as serious threats rather than one more negotiation strategy.

> Man: This is nonnegotiable. [A bluff.]

> Woman: Fine, then. Have it your way. [She accepts the bluff as reality.]

This may be a way of saying that women tend to attach meanings to words and assume that male speakers do as well. In this example, the woman speaker believes that the man knows what "nonnegotiable" means and chooses that word sincerely to describe his position. If the man knows that his position is negotiable but chooses to dissemble, are we to praise his strategy and recommend it to both genders? In George Orwell's fine phrase, "The great enemy of language is insincerity." Women have much to teach about integrity in saying what you mean and meaning what you say.

---

[4] Senge, Peter. *The Fifth Discipline: The Art and Practice of the Learning Organization.* New York: Doubleday, 1994..

What men and women say is not always what they mean. Listen to subtle expressions of attitude and emotion and pay attention to nonverbal signs to determine the complete meaning of a statement.

INSIGHT 22

Your Turn

Describe a time when a person's words to you revealed only a small portion of the complete meaning they were trying to communicate. How did you go about discovering the full intent of their communication?

4. In decision making, women are more likely to downplay their certainty; men are more likely to downplay their doubts.

Woman: In making this recommendation, I think I've covered every base—at least the ones I'm aware of.

Man: I make this recommendation with complete confidence.

This language tendency on the part of women is sometimes portrayed as an inability to stand strong as a confident decision maker. It can just as easily be regarded and valued as a reluctance to bluff the audience or to assume a posture of confidence that is neither felt by the speaker nor supported by the facts. Women, by their language of qualification as exemplified here, may be providing a necessary caution against the male tendency toward exaggeration and bravado. In effect, women are telling it like it is: "I'm not entirely sure about my conclusions and I'm not going to pretend otherwise. To do so would be lying to you and, ultimately, empowering myself at your expense."

5. Women tend to lead by making suggestions and explaining those suggestions in terms of the good of the team. Men are more likely to lead by giving orders, with explanations (if any) based on rationales related to project goals.

Woman: Let's proceed by dividing into teams. I think we can make the most of our individual talents by working with one another in smaller groups.

Man: We're going to break into teams to divide up the workload and meet our deadlines.

Modern teams obviously require both approaches to planning and decision making as a way of dealing with rapidly changing business conditions. For every occasion when the team must be nourished and encouraged there is also a circumstance when someone has to make decisions without consensus (or relying on a trust bond that already exists within the group). The important point is that neither style is dysfunctional; both can be useful on teams to serve different but complementary goals.

6. Women tend to apologize even when they have done nothing wrong. Men tend to avoid apologies as signs of weakness or concession.

> Woman: I'm sorry, but I have to read you this e-mail that just arrived from the boss.

> Man: Listen up. The boss just sent this e-mail.

In this case, only the most rigid literalist would interpret the phrase, "I'm sorry" as an apology for a mistake of some kind. These words instead reveal a recognition that the listener's feelings may be bruised by the ensuing message, and that the speaker is not unaware of or unresponsive to those feelings. In this way, the communication patterns of women tend to insert emotional buffers into sometimes turbulent business life. What on the surface may appear to be unjustified apologizing is, at a deeper level, an effort to humanize the team and soften harsh effects.

INSIGHT 23	Apologies and equivocations do not necessarily indicate guilt or a perception of wrongdoing on the part of the speaker. These phrases may be a way of attempting to deal gently with an uncomfortable moment or situation.

Your Turn	
Consider your own use of apology phrases such as "I'm sorry, but . . ." or "Excuse me" beyond their literal meanings. Try to paraphrase exactly what you are attempting to communicate by the use of these phrases.	

7. Women tend to accept blame as a way of smoothing awkward situations. Men tend to ignore blame or place it elsewhere.

> Woman: I probably didn't welcome our Japanese visitors exactly as I should have, but I tried to be gracious and sincere.

> Man: I met the Japanese visitors at the airport. Next time someone should tell me when and how to bow.

Teams require accountability, but it is hardly present in the male language pattern illustrated here. The woman is clearly accepting responsibility both for what went right and what went wrong in her efforts to greet the Japanese visitors. The man, by contrast, seeks to avoid personal account-ability and instead to pass it on to a vague "someone" in the organization. When less-than-ideal situations in business occur, the language habits of women may be more likely to depict accurately the accountability involved.

8. Women tend to temper criticism with positive buffers. Men tend to give criticism directly.

> Woman: You're doing a great job on this report, but you may want to look at page eight one more time. At least see what you think.

> Man: Fix page eight, then let me reread your report one final time before we send it upstairs.

An awareness of the listener's feelings is not a bad thing for team rela-tionships. In this woman's example, the speaker tries to preserve the relation-ship while changing the behavior. The man seems more willing to sacrifice or at least risk the relationship for the sake of behavior. That choice leads di-rectly, on many teams, to low morale and excessive turnover of membership.

9. Women tend to insert unnecessary and unwarranted "thank you's" in conversations. Men tend to avoid thanks as a sign of weakness.

> Woman: Thanks anyway, but I don't think I want to trade my parking place with Jack.

> Man: No, I don't want to trade for Jack's spot.

The facade of thanks is only part of a complex architecture of courtesy and civility that women may tend to prefer in the team environment. By con-trast, the apparent tone of the male response portrays the team environment as an arena for confrontation, victory, defeat, and perhaps bullying.

Every manager must deliver constructive criticism, often hourly or daily. Your own way of delivering such criticism may be influenced by your gender.	**INSIGHT 24**

Your Turn

Write down how you prefer to receive criticism of your work behavior when such criticism is necessary. Then describe how one or two recent supervisors have chosen to deliver perfor-mance evaluations or other forms of constructive criticism. Did their approach to delivering criti-cism meet with your approval? If so, how did you feel in receiving the criticism and what was the result? If not, how did you feel in receiving the criticism and what was the result?

10. Women tend to ask, "What do you think?" to build consensus. Men often perceive the question to be a sign of incompetence and lack of confidence.

> Woman: What do you think about dividing my office into a work area and a waiting area?

> Man [thinks]: It's her office. Can't she decide what she wants to do?

Let's assume that the woman in this case knows full well what she wants to do with her office. Her question is not a solicitation of permission (although the man takes it as such) nor a sign that she can't make her own decisions. Instead, it is another demonstration of the tendency we have already observed in women's language patterns to gather input and weigh opinions before acting.

11. Women tend to mix business talk with talk about their personal lives and expect other women to do so as well. Men mix business talk with banter about sports, politics, or jokes (many of them sexually oriented).

> Woman: I don't mind traveling to Cincinnati, but it will mean finding overnight care for our baby.

> Man: If I do go to Cincinnati, I'm taking an afternoon off to see a ball game. That's the least they can do.

This question is worth asking: Which gender is expressing most truthfully and accurately the impact team and business responsibilities have on personal life? Let's assume that the man in this case is a father and that he, no less than the working woman, has family matters to consider in arranging his business trip. He too must make provision for children, pets, and so forth. The point is that the woman tends to discuss with others how business duties influence her personal life. The man is reluctant to do so. Businesses probably operate best knowing what problems, obstacles, and burdens their employees face. By knowing an employee's circumstances, the business can adapt for win-win solutions.

12. Women feel that men aren't direct enough in telling them what they (women) are doing right. Men feel that women aren't direct enough in telling them what they (men) are doing wrong.

> Woman: I don't know how you feel about my work. [This is a request for more feedback.]

> Man: Just tell me right out if you don't like what I'm doing. [This is a request to avoid mixed signals.]

Feedback is a business buzzword that refuses to fade, perhaps because of its importance to employee motivation and quality management, including that of teams. Both genders in this example are asking for feedback, but the woman's way of asking is more in line with the 360-degree-feedback systems currently used for performance evaluations at all levels of teamwork. The woman's communication pattern allows for the possibility that feedback may include both positive and negative aspects, that is, the full range of evaluation. The man's communication pattern closes the door to praise almost entirely and solicits only negative feedback.

Soliciting the opinions of others ("What do you think?") often is not an invitation to provide specific answers so much as an invitation to join in discussion and to offer an emotional response of some kind.	**INSIGHT 25**

Your Turn
Recall a recent conversation with a member of the opposite sex in which you seemed to have different goals for the conversation or in some way "talked past" one another. As you reflect on that conversation, what do you believe the conversational expectations of the other person were? What were your conversational expectations?

13. Women bring up complaints and troubles with one another as a means of arousing sympathy and building rapport. Men bring up problems only when they want to hear solutions.

Woman: Our problem at home is just not having enough time with each other. I get home just as Bob is leaving for his job.

Man: We haven't been out to a show for months. Where do you find babysitters?

Sharing problems is not just an effort to build rapport and arouse sympathy. In addition, and perhaps more crucially, it is an effort to understand pain and thereby alleviate it. The woman's communication pattern assumes that the group may have insights and experiences that will enlighten the nature of the pain or frustration at hand. The man's communication pattern is cynical about the ability of the surrounding group to provide indepth perspectives or resonant ideas. The woman wants help in understanding the problem; the man wants help in postponing the problem.

14. Women's humor tends to be self-mocking. Men's humor tends to be razzing, teasing, and mock-hostile attacking.

Woman: So I said in my charming way, "You forgot to plug it in."

Man: So I said, "Did you notice anything strange about the cord lying on the floor?"

Freud wrote at length about "tendency humor"—our effort to disguise in humor what we really want to communicate, but dare not directly. The tendency of the male communication pattern illustrated here is to emphasize the person's stupidity or foolishness. By contrast, the person making the comment is to be seen as superior and smarter. The woman defuses this potential power play in her softened version of the verbal transaction. She recognizes that the person may feel insecure and awkward about the incident, and so consciously lowers her own status by self-mocking humor to avoid a threat to the relationship.

15. Women tend to give directions in indirect ways, a technique that may be perceived by men as confusing, less confident, or manipulative.

Woman: You can handle this account any way you want, but taking him out to lunch might be a possibility. Or meet in his office. Whatever you think. Lunch, though, might be the way to go.

Man [thinks]: Is she telling me to take him out to lunch or not? Is she setting me up for an I-told-you-so if I don't do it her way? And what is her way?

Teams make much of empowerment, which can only take place when the decision maker has options. In this example, the woman's communication pattern is conducive to empowerment because it leaves the decision maker free to choose, learn, and grow within a range of options. The man's apparent preference for a command style of management may allow short-term efficiencies, but does not encourage empowerment with its allied benefits of creativity, motivation, and loyalty.

INSIGHT 26	Humor often disguises messages that others are trying to share with us. Seeing through the humor to the underlying message can be a good way of determining the true nature of your relationship with the other person.

Your Turn

Think of someone in your work or social life who uses humor, perhaps in a mocking way, to say something to you and other people. Write down an approximate translation of what that person is usually trying to communicate by such humor. Why do you believe the person uses humor to disguise those messages?

16. When women and men gather in a team setting, women tend to change their communication styles to adapt to the presence of the men. Women also practice "silent applause" by smiling often, agreeing with others often, and giving more nonverbal signals of attentiveness than do men.

Audience adaptation is highly recommended in virtually all communication guides and textbooks. The apparent fact that women change their communication behaviors based on their audience is not a sign of uncertainty, deceit, or weakness. Instead, it is an effort to relate successfully.

17. Women in positions of team leadership tend to be less accustomed to dealing with conflict and attack than are men.

Woman: Why is everyone mad at me?

Man: This is an unpopular decision, but I've got to make it.

As consensus builders, women respond quickly and vocally to signs that consensus is failing and that relationships are threatened. For generations this behavior has been interpreted negatively: "If you can't stand the heat, stay out of the kitchen." It can just as well be interpreted positively for the purposes of modern teams. Women are no less tough for recognizing and responding to conflict and attack. It can be argued that they are all the more tough for their willingness to confront and deal with those forces rather than stoically or stubbornly ignoring them.

18. Women tend to be referred to more often by their first name than are men, sometimes as a sign of respect for women and sometimes as a sign of presumed familiarity or intimacy.

Man: Get Smith, Underwood, Connors, and Jill to go along with you on the sales call.

The use of the woman's first name in this example may or may not be a subtle way for the man to minimize the woman's professionalism. He may feel more gallant in calling women by their first names. As a team leader, however, he should choose one form of address or the other and apply it consistently to both genders.

19. Men tend to be uncomfortable with female peers, particularly those who may threaten their power.

Working for a woman is uncomfortable for many men, primarily because they misunderstand the communication patterns explained throughout this chapter. The male employee may complain about the woman boss's seeming lack of direct supervision and mixed messages, whereas the woman boss may simultaneously complain about the male employee's unwillingness to discuss problems openly, to work well with others on the team, and to share ideas.

20. Men tend to perceive a group of women in conversation as wasting time or hatching a plot of some kind. Women tend to perceive a group of men in conversation as doing business or working out power relations through bonding and joking.

These impressions from a distance of gender-exclusive groups tell volumes about the core misunderstandings between male and female members of a team. Interestingly, women credit men with more positive activities (doing business, etc.) than is the reverse (wasting time, hatching plots). Are women more sanguine about their fellow team members than are men? Do women tend to see the corporate glass as half full and men to see it as half empty?

INSIGHT 27	One's comfort level in working for or with members of the opposite gender can help or hinder career success. It is important to understand one's feelings about the role of gender in interpersonal relations.

Your Turn

Briefly describe in writing your own experiences and feelings about working for a member of the opposite gender. If you prefer, describe the attitudes of someone who has strong feelings (pro or con) about working for a member of the opposite sex. Explain their attitudes to the best of your ability.

Summing Up

Balancing the personal qualities, expertise, experience, and other factors of team members is important in achieving a harmonious team that discusses issues fully and reaches decisions only after gathering a wide range of data. An evaluation of personality types can be useful in establishing this balance, but such personality information should not be applied too narrowly or literally. In attempting to balance the influence and interaction of men and women on a productive team, a team leader or manager must bear in mind many communication differences associated with gender. Communication on the team can be improved if all members are aware of and respect the value of these communication differences.

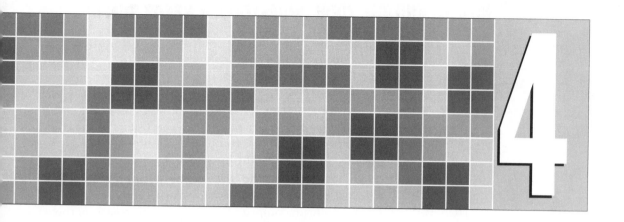

Becoming a Team Member and a Team Leader

GOALS

- Discover how to establish teams within an organization.
- Prepare for effective membership skills on a team.
- Learn techniques for leading teams.

In the best of all worlds, successful teams are already a well-established tradition within your company. There's a place waiting for you on a team. In that case you may want to skim this chapter, because it assumes that this is not the best of all worlds, and that you may have to work for—even create—your own place on a productive team.

HOW TO KNOW IF YOUR ORGANIZATION NEEDS TEAMS

Let's say that you are now associated with a company or organization that makes little or no use of teams. Is there a reason why it should? Yes, if it experiences any of the following circumstances:

- Projects, documents, and other major tasks are done by one or two individuals, then distributed for significant revision by others in the company. (A team could speed this process by putting all those involved into the development loop from the beginning.)
- Political factions vie for resources and distrust the work product of any one faction. (If departments or divisions within the company do not share turf comfortably, a team comprised of members from each of these groups may ease tensions and give more credibility and acceptance to work products developed by the team.)
- Employee turnover is high because workers know few other people in the company and have little reason to stay beyond the paycheck. (Human relationships are fostered in a team environment—and those relationships can dramatically decrease employee turnover.)
- The company's work product requires input from several specialized skill areas. (A team can combine these skill areas and afford a measure of cross-training in the process.)

INSIGHT 28	The team approach to work is more appropriate in some organizational environments than in others. To decide whether teams are advantageous to it, a company must evaluate its work goals and culture.

Your Turn	
Think of a company or organization (perhaps one to which you now belong) where the team approach to work appears to be a good idea. Discuss reasons to support your opinion.	

PUTTING TOGETHER YOUR CASE FOR A TEAM

If you find yourself having to propose team-based work to your manager, here are the bases you will want to touch in preparing to make your case.

1. Make a list of projects, documents, presentations, and other company tasks that could be accomplished with higher quality in less time and at

lower cost by a team. (If no such tasks are available in your company, the chances are slim that management will see the need for teams.)

2. With your manager's approval, circulate your list of possible team projects to a wide cross-section of those likely to be chosen for company teams. Survey their interests, including questions about any reservations they may have about team work. (For example, some workers may wonder how they will be evaluated for raises and promotions if they serve on a team. Will their individual effort count, or will they be judged along with the entire team?)

3. Compile the results of your findings in a concise report addressed to management. You should accompany your report with a cover memo summarizing your case for teams (see the examples that follow in this chapter).

You may be addressing executives who have already had good experiences with teams in other companies or have heard good things about teams from peer companies. In that case, your memo and report will probably gain easy acceptance. If your senior management is sour on teams from past experience, you may find that your memo and report lead to a number of meetings with management, where you will have to sell your idea more thoroughly.

Upper management must often be convinced of the need for teams by the potential team members themselves.	**INSIGHT 29**

	Your Turn
Assume that you wanted to form a team within a company or organization that you know well. Describe in specific steps how you would go about getting authorization to form the team.	

A SAMPLE COMMUNICATION TO MANAGEMENT REGARDING TEAM FORMATION

To: Morton Evans
Executive Vice President
XYZ Corporation

From: (you)
Subject: Advantages of Forming Work Teams

I'm pleased to attach my report, "Attitudes and Opportunities regarding Teams at XYZ Corporation." It makes the case that employees working in teams can accomplish corporate assignments more quickly, more affordably, and with more quality than under the present sole-worker arrangement. The report also summarizes a survey of 100 employees, 92 percent of which believe that team-based work would be good for the company, good for their development as employees, and good for product improvements. After you have had a chance to read this report, I would appreciate an opportunity to meet with you to learn about your perspective on the establishment of work teams at XYZ and to talk about ways that any obstacles to teamwork can be removed. Thank you in advance for your interest in what I believe to be a promising development for the company.

Your communication, of course, may be worded differently as you try to match your argument to the nature and needs of your audience. In any case, it's a good idea to write down your argument even if you plan to deliver it orally to your boss. The process of writing down your ideas gives you a chance to see how well they hang together, how well they are supported, and to what degree they can be streamlined to make your point with more impact.

INSIGHT 30	Written or oral requests for the formation of teams must show why the team approach to work has advantages over other approaches.

Your Turn

What three points (you may have more) would you make in a memo to upper management in your efforts to win approval of the formation of a work team? Use any company or other organization you know well.

PREPARING FOR TEAM MEMBERSHIP

The boss says "yes." You realize from your survey of employees, however, that their eagerness to participate in teams is not matched by their preparation to do so. You may feel that you need a brush-up of team member skills yourself.

Here, then, is the outline of a boot camp of sorts for those who want to work well as team members. This list can serve as the backbone of a training program in your company for potential team participants.

Before becoming a member of a team, an employee must know how to

- listen to others
- work without close direction

- give and take constructive criticism
- participate in efficient discussions
- understand the nature of consensus decision making
- work well with others
- share credit and blame as a group rather than as an individual
- consider the welfare of the team in your words and actions to outsiders
- contribute expertise without flaunting it

The skills necessary for a strong team member may be somewhat different than the skills required for a strong sole contributor to an organization.	**INSIGHT 31**

Your Turn
Using the qualities just listed, evaluate your own abilities as a team member. Where do your strengths lie and where do you need improvement? For the area(s) of improvement, tell how you could go about becoming more skilled.

PREPARING TO LEAD A TEAM

Every team established by management will probably have a leader, usually drawn from among the ranks of the team members themselves. Some companies obey a seniority principle in selecting team leaders. Others award the position to the highest paid or most degreed worker in the group. The wisest companies, however, pick the person who has the best leadership skills. If you intend to be that person—or to be able to recognize him or her on your team—here's a concise summary of the qualities most often sought in team leaders. This individual must be able to

- withhold personal ideas and judgment long enough for others on the team to have their say
- listen with interest and respect even to ideas and opinions that differ significantly from their own
- direct traffic in discussion without playing favorites
- draw out quieter members of the team and hold back more vociferous members as necessary
- keep discussion moving in a fruitful direction, with an eye toward reaching stages of agreement that will eventually underpin a decision
- build consensus rather than forcing close votes

- focus the team, as often as required, on its short- and long-term goals
- defuse conflict among team members by distinguishing between ideas and personalities, redirecting comments, and using humor as appropriate
- be an advocate for the team in its negotiation for resources, personnel, facilities, and support
- be a liaison for the team with upper management
- be a cheerleader for the team, with a firm belief in the ability of the team to achieve its goals

A team leader doesn't need to have "the right stuff," if that phrase implies some kind of heroic courage and wisdom. Good team leadership is much more a matter of learned skills applied consistently—doing things right.

INSIGHT 32	The skills necessary for strong team leadership go beyond those required for strong team membership. A team leader should not be chosen simply because he or she has been a good team member.

Your Turn	
Using the leadership qualities just listed, evaluate your own abilities as a team leader. Where do your strengths lie and in what area(s) do you need improvement? For the areas named for improvement, tell how you would go about becoming more skilled.	

ACTIVITIES FOR THE FIRST TEAM MEETING

So far so good. With the help of your company's training department, you've prepared team members and team leaders. You're now ready to kick off your first team meeting—a marketing team, let's say, with responsibility for investigating and recommending new sales opportunities for the company.

Your first team meeting is crucial in setting the agreed-upon ground rules, goals, and methods of operation for the team. It's a good idea to allow team members to get to know one another before any substantive issues are discussed or decided upon. The typical "let's each introduce ourselves" approach gives each member a chance to speak briefly, but does not allow opportunity for relationships to develop. Therefore, consider one of the following icebreakers:

1. Team members are divided into pairs, with person A interviewing and gathering notes on person B, and vice versa. After 20 minutes or so of such paired conversation, person A introduces person B to the team, then person B

introduces person A. The process continues until all team members have been introduced. The team leader should include himself or herself in this activity so as not to seem aloof from or superior to other team members. In the case of an odd number of team members, one group of three can form, with person A interviewing person B who interviews person C who interviews person A.

2. Each member of the team is given a few minutes to call to mind a brief "impress us—depress us" set of experiences to tell the group. For example, a member might decide to talk about recently having twins on the "impress us" side, then tell about the cost of diapers on the "depress us" side. Another team member may point to some impressive achievement in the company, then talk about a recent depressor such as a speeding ticket or car problem. This good-natured activity gives members not only a chance to tell something positive about themselves but also to poke a bit of self-directed humor at something less positive. In virtually all teams where this activity has been tried, a great deal of laughter accompanies the disclosures of team members. If time allows, team members can ask questions after each person's turn at speaking.

3. Each member takes a minute or so to tell what he or she would do if they won the lottery. Because this activity takes the focus off business, it gives members a chance to get to know one another as people. This form of self-introduction invites a mixture of humor and serious disclosure and can be accompanied by questions from the group.

No matter what icebreaking activity you decide to use, make every effort to avoid the drill sergeant approach to the first meeting, in which one person drones on while team members sit silent and become increasingly sullen about the team experience.

Team members must get to know and trust one another before open discussion of work issues can be successfully undertaken.	**INSIGHT 33**

Your Turn

Recall the first meeting of a team on which you served. How did team members get to know one another? If the members knew each other before joining the team, how was the first meeting spent? Looking back, would you have used this time differently in any way if you had been the team leader?

WRITING AN INFORMAL AGENDA FOR TEAM MEETINGS

As a general rule, team meetings do not follow the same rigid agenda or rules of order used by standing committees of companies and other organizations. It's rare indeed to find a team that abides strictly by Robert's Rules of Order in conducting discussion and making decisions. On the other hand, teams require some organization for their meetings and a reasonable degree of prior notice about the topics to be discussed.

Several days before the team meeting, the team leader should contact team members to gather suggestions for agenda items, announcements, and other matters for the meeting. The team leader compiles these ideas into an informal agenda that should be sent to each member with enough advance notice to allow calendaring the meeting and preparing for the topics to be discussed. Of course, many teams have a fixed time each week or other period for their meeting.

The goal of this informal agenda is to keep discussion from becoming chaotic or imbalanced. Devoting most of the team meeting to a relatively trivial item wastes not only the meeting at hand, but also pushes forward more and more weighty topics to future meetings, where insufficient time may be available to give them their due. An informal agenda structures and paces the work of the team without imposing a rigid schedule or process that detracts from the nature and advantages of the team approach.

Here is an example of an informal agenda for a meeting of a marketing team composed of six members:

Weekly Meeting for February 8, 200_, 10:00 A.M. to 12:00 P.M.,
Conference Room 323.
Marketing Team: A. Williams, C. Trent, G. Chung, H. Evans, E. Ramirez.
Contact for questions and input: G. Chung, ext. 9824.

Scheduled topics for discussion:

1. Discussion and possible decision on partnering with C-tronics—30 min. Overview of issues: C. Trent

2. Review of advertising media recommendations—30 min. Overview of issues: H. Evans

3. Investigation of vendor marketing models—60 min. Overview of issues: E. Ramirez

By this simple agenda, sent to participants several business days before the meeting, the team leader—G. Chung in this case—sets up the team meeting for success in several ways. First, the burden for introducing each of the main topics is taken off the team leader and distributed to the team members themselves. They have ample notice from the team leader to prepare their remarks for the meeting. This distribution of responsibility has the added value of building the participation and leadership skills of the members. Second, the topics for the meeting are published so that members can think about them before the meeting, not just during the meeting. Finally, a time limit is recommended (though not insisted upon) for each topic so that more important or more complicated topics receive an appropriate amount of time for discussion. If the team discovers at the meeting that a particular topic is taking more time than anticipated, the members can agree to redistribute the time limits suggested on the informal agenda.

Teams usually do not require a formal agenda, but they can gain advantages from an informal description of topics and responsibilities distributed well in advance of meetings.	**INSIGHT 34**

	Your Turn
Think about a team on which you now serve or have served. Does the team make use of an agenda of any kind? If so, describe and evaluate it. If not, explain why an informal agenda would or would not be appropriate for your team.	

TAKING NOTES OR MINUTES FOR TEAM MEETINGS

In the same way that agendas for team meetings are usually less formal than agendas for traditional committees, so the notes or minutes for team meetings are less formal in format but not less accurate in description and detail. A team usually does not have a non-team member (such as a secretary) present to take notes. Nor does one of the team members opt out of discussion for the sake of keeping the minutes. Instead, team members can take turns writing up the nature of discussion and decisions for distribution to all members after the meeting. The goal of these less formal notes is to record what the team considered and decided, not to present a blow-by-blow description of who said what to whom. Team minutes are usually distributed within 48 hours of the meeting. In some organizations, teams keep their notes or minutes confidential so that interim team opinions are not misinterpreted by the rest of the organization as final judgments. In other companies, teams use their minutes as a way of keeping the rest of the workforce, especially upper management, informed of their activities on a week-by-week basis.

Here is an example of minutes for the marketing team's February 8 meeting (see previous agenda):

Minutes for weekly meeting for February 8, 200_, 10:00 A.M. to 12:00 P.M.,
Conference Room 323.
Marketing Team: Attending were A. Williams, C. Trent, G. Chung, H.
Evans, E. Ramirez.
Please direct questions, comments, or corrections to G. Chung, ext. 9824.

Topics discussed:

1. Possibility of partnering with C-tronics on magazine advertising: C. Trent presented an analysis of pros and cons. Discussion focused on C-tronics's low name recognition for our customer base. Decision postponed until after a presentation by a C-tronics representative scheduled for February 15.

2. Advertising media recommendations: H. Evans reviewed team findings for television and internet advertising. Team unanimously agreed to recommendation contained in supplement A.

3. Investigation of vendor marketing models: E. Ramirez presented four vendor models for discussion. Team concluded discussion of models 1 and 2; discussion of the remaining models was sent forward to the next weekly meeting.

Meeting notes taken by: A. Williams

INSIGHT 35	Teams require a permanent record of their topics, discussion, and decisions.

Your Turn

Think of a team on which you now serve or have served. Describe and evaluate any system of notes, minutes, or other record keeping used by your team. If your team uses no such system, describe a form of notes or minutes that you believe would be helpful to your team and organization.

KEEPING THE TEAM INFORMED BETWEEN MEETINGS

The team leader makes pertinent information available as it arises between meetings. However, the responsibility for gathering and distributing such information should not fall to the team leader alone. Each team member has the ongoing task of keeping in touch with the rest of the team between meetings, sending insights as they occur rather than saving them up for a meeting, and gathering information that may prove useful to the team. In this way the team avoids meetings characterized by lectures that transfer knowledge to team members, and instead makes it possible for knowledge to be discussed. Only by getting knowledge between meetings can the team reserve the meeting time itself for an evaluation of that knowledge.

	INSIGHT 36
The work of a team does not begin and end with its meetings. Team leaders and members make an effort to acquire and distribute insights and information between meetings so that meeting time can be used for discussion and decision making.	

Your Turn
Think of a team on which you now serve or have served. Describe what members typically do between meetings with regard to the work of the team. Make any recommendations you wish for ways in which that between-meeting time could be better used to the team's advantage.

Summing Up

Teams become valuable to organizations only when team members are prepared for team participation and leadership. The skills that make for a successful team often require training; the competencies that make for a productive single contributor in the organization may be quite different from the abilities that make for a good team member or leader. By using informal meeting agendas and notes or minutes, teams organize their work and record progress.

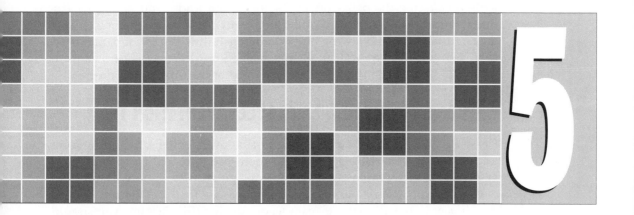

Observing Team Leadership Skills at Work

GOALS

- Understand the minute-by-minute decisions and adjustments made by team leaders during a team meeting.

- Grasp the range of options available to team leaders in "directing traffic" for team discussions.

- Model successful behaviors of team leaders.

According to the often-quoted Confucian adage, "I hear and I forget; I see and I remember; I do and I understand." Although we cannot reach through the words on this page to guide what you do as a team leader or member, we can create an extended scenario—a team soap opera, if you will—illustrating the behaviors of a skilled team leader and taking you inside the team leader's head to understand why those behavior choices were made. Although the following bit of drama including the use of names is entirely fictional, it may recall moments from your own experience on a team when the behavior of the team leader helped or hurt the team's progress.

WELCOME TO THE NEW EMPLOYEE ORIENTATION TEAM

Please assume, in the following scenario, that five members, including team leader Kate Conway, have gathered for their second meeting to discuss how best to orient new employees to the culture, procedures, resources, and rules of the company. All names and circumstances are fictitious. To understand the choices Kate will make as team leader during this meeting, you should meet the other members of the team:

> Jose Velasquez, 40, is a mid-level personnel manager who has worked for the company for 5 years. He tends to be rather quiet during team meetings, speaking up only when he feels he is on the majority side of any issue. Jose is a people person and does whatever he can to make others on the team feel comfortable. He becomes uncomfortable himself when team members appear to be irritated or angry with one another.
>
> Linda Johnson, 29, is a manager in the accounting department of the company. Although she regularly takes on new employees as her subordinates, she does not understand why her boss insisted that she serve on this orientation team. She has often pointed out that she is an accountant and does not have direct expertise in personnel matters. She does have strong opinions, however, and often expresses them as final judgments rather than suggestions.
>
> George Han, 52, is one of the company's lawyers. His primary interest lies in making sure that new employees know the rules, procedures, and guidelines contained in the employee handbook. Although he gets along well with the rest of the team, he has little patience for orientation proposals that have to do with company culture, motivation, and a welcoming entry into the employee family.
>
> Vic Benson, 26, is a recruitment specialist who has worked for the company for only 1 year. He is a high-energy, slap-on-the-back person who seems in a perpetual rush. Vic frequently arrives late at meetings; in discussion, he tends to rush to early conclusions and decisions. He is always one of the first to speak up on any topic and often cuts others off in mid-sentence to insert his own opinions.

THE MEETING BEGINS

Team Leader Kate: It's a few minutes after 10:00, so let's get started. Vic obviously isn't here yet, but I don't think we should wait any longer. [Members exchange glances; they know Vic's habits.] I've asked Jose to give us a quick overview of our main topic today. Jose? [Kate selects Jose for these opening remarks partly to remove herself from the spotlight and also to get Jose involved in participation. She knows that if Jose speaks up early he will be more likely to contribute throughout the rest of the meeting.]

Jose: Sure. The main thing we have to discuss today, and I guess make some decisions about, is whether we want the new employees—let's say 40 of them or so—to meet as a group for orientation or in smaller sets of maybe 8 or 10. Personally, I don't see where it makes that much difference because they are all going to get the same information anyway.

[At this point Vic bursts into the room, papers bulging from a file folder in his hand. He grabs an empty chair at the table and gives an "oops!" look to Kate and other members. At this point Kate has some interesting choices. She could say something direct about Vic's lateness. If she does, Vic may get to the meeting on time in the future, but may harbor a lingering grudge against Kate for what he may see as an insult in front of others. Kate also wonders if a stern comment to Vic at this point may define her leadership style incorrectly for the rest of the team, some of whom aren't yet entirely on board with the work and spirit of the group. Kate chooses to say nothing about Vic's late arrival and moves ahead with the meeting.]

Kate: Thanks, Jose. Vic, we're discussing whether to orient new employees in a big group or smaller groups. [To the rest of the team:] What are your thoughts?" [Kate could have structured her opening question more specifically and directively: "Let's first come up with advantages of the large group approach, then look at its disadvantages. We then can do the same thing with the small group approach." She doesn't take this option, however, because this is only the team's second meeting. In her judgment, the team needs a sense of ownership with respect to how it organizes its work and discusses topics.]

Vic [eagerly]:   What do you mean by smaller groups? [Kate at this point is tempted to tell Vic, "If you had been here on time you would know we're talking about 8 to 10 people in a group." Instead, she turns over this disciplinary role to the team itself by looking to other members for a reply.]

George [pointedly to Vic]:   Jose opened the meeting by suggesting that there would be 8 to 10 people in a small group. That sounds about right to me. [Vic appears ready to talk back to George, but Kate heads him off by addressing a question to Linda from accounting.] Linda, your department sees a lot of these new employees. What are your thoughts about the question of group size?

Linda: All I notice is that my new employees seem pretty isolated for the first few weeks. I'm no personnel expert, but there must be ways to make them feel part of the company more quickly. [Kate recognizes that Linda hasn't addressed the question of group size directly. Kate could repeat the question, but guesses wisely that Linda is waiting for Jose to weigh in as the personnel guru on the team. Kate allows a pause to see if Jose will speak up.]

Vic: Well, I recruited a lot of these people and they don't have social problems, if that's what Linda is saying: They were all very friendly to me. Maybe it's just the environment in accounting. [Kate sees Linda start to bristle.]

Kate [directing the team]:   Let's stick to the question of group size for a few minutes. Thoughts? [Kate looks at the noncombatants, Jose and George, to give Linda a moment to cool off.]

George: We've always done orientation in a big group and got it done in only a couple days. I don't see any reason to make more work for ourselves.

Jose: But George, have you been satisfied with the results of that kind of orientation? I mean, are they really "oriented" from your perspective? [Kate lets this dialogue continue. It is the kind of team thinking and interaction that she wants to encourage. Jose is getting George to examine his remarks, but not in an attacking way.]

George: Well, they don't know what they should about the employee handbook—

Vic [cuts George off abruptly]:   That handbook needs a complete rewriting and—

Kate [has to restrain Vic here to keep the discussion on track]:   Just a second, Vic. Let George finish his thought.

George: I was just saying that new employees aren't very well prepared when it comes to understanding the policies and procedures of the company.

Jose: So maybe we can improve by putting them in smaller groups. [George shrugs his shoulders as if to say, "Maybe so."]

Kate: Well, let's start there. What advantages do we see in using smaller groups for orientation? [Kate looks toward group members who haven't spoken recently.]

Linda: In smaller groups at least we would have a chance to get to know them individually and see if they have questions or misunderstandings. I mean, in a group of 40 it's just lecture, lecture, lecture for 2 days straight.

Jose: That's right. People do tend to speak up with their questions a lot more in small groups.

Vic: I think they could get to know each other easier in small groups than in one big group. [Kate spots a leadership opportunity here. She can give Vic some kind of praise for making a positive contribution to the discussion instead of his usual off-track remarks. Kate also sees that Vic is starting to support Linda's position; Kate wants to seize this opportunity to heal the bad interpersonal chemistry between these two.]

Kate: That's a good point, Vic. So the second reason has to do with social-ization. That supports what you were saying, Linda—

Linda: Right. If my new employees knew even a handful of people to have coffee or lunch with from the beginning, they would be a lot better off and probably more productive in their first few weeks. [Kate senses that the ball is rolling nicely now. Group members are motivated to think of more positive rea-sons to support the small group approach to orientation. Kate decides to get a couple more advantages out on the table before raising the question—or, bet-ter, getting the group to raise the question—of disadvantages to the small group approach. Kate is aware of GroupThink, and knows that good decisions come only from seeing the whole picture.]

George: I guess another advantage would be dividing people up according to which department they will be going to. If Linda's people need to get to know each other, we could put them together into one of the orientation groups.

Jose: No problem. George, should we do the same thing with new employ-ees and interns who will be working with your people in administration?

George: I don't see why not. Our group may be smaller than Linda's, of course. [In George's comment, Kate hears the first note of the disadvantages of the small group approach. She decides to steer the group gently toward a consideration of those disadvantages, but not before solidifying the four advan-tages in everyone's minds.]

Kate: So, summing up for a minute, we seem to feel that small groups would provide better orientation toward the employee handbook, let people ask ques-tions and make comments, get to know one another, and be divided according to where they're going to work in the company. Did I get it right? [Kate waits for verbal or nonverbal approval from the team before moving ahead.] But George, you started to touch on a disadvantage . . .

George: I'm not sure if it's a disadvantage, but the groups won't all be the same size.

Vic: Sounds like a disadvantage to me. If one group has three people in it, they will either feel they're special or that they're being singled out for some reason.

Linda [more willing again to work comfortably with Vic]:   If I were in a group of three people and I knew others were in groups of 10 or so, I would feel per-secuted. New employees always seem to see the glass as half empty instead of half full.

Kate [wanting to proceed now to a careful examination of disadvantages]:   So one disadvantage may be the different sizes of groups. Any other disadvantages?

[Kate can think of several herself, but knows that these points need to come from the group itself if a consensus decision is eventually to be reached.]

Jose: I'm totally in favor of the small group approach. [Kate doesn't want to rush to judgment so quickly.]

Kate: No matter how we each feel about it right now, let's do the "due diligence" thing and at least think through any disadvantages. Jose, from a personnel point of view, do small groups pose any problem in this kind of situation? [Kate is trying to keep Jose from steering the team away from a complete analysis and discussion of the topic. She doesn't want to appear to be chiding Jose, so she gives him an implicit compliment by referring to his personnel expertise while at the same time guiding him toward the track of discussion she wants to continue.]

Jose: There's a ton of research on small group behaviors. The only thing I can think of could be some kind of us-against-them attitude on the part of the groups. For example, if we put Linda's people all in a group from day one, they are never going to feel part of the same team as George's new people or, for that matter, the new employees coming to work with Vic and me.

Kate [thinks she has to make the point crystal clear]:   So, I'm hearing that people may identify too much with their small group rather than the company. Any other disadvantages? [Kate doesn't direct this question to Jose because he has already indicated that his well is dry when it comes to other responses. Kate knows that pressing him will only lead to his embarrassment at being put on the spot, and may lead Jose to return to his nonparticipative behavior.]

Vic: It's going to cost personnel more to run four sections of 10 people than one section of 40 people. Linda can probably estimate for us. [Kate's work in keeping Vic and Linda from sniping at each other has paid off. Vic is learning to turn to others on the team for their expertise rather than blustering on about his own opinions. Kate could compliment Vic again, but decides to do so only nonverbally so as not to appear to be laying it on too thick or patronizing Vic.]

Linda: Just a rough estimate, really. Small groups will probably cost about 50 percent more than doing orientation the old way with one big group.

George: Now there's a disadvantage for you. [The group chuckles, but Kate picks up the serious point.]

Kate: So our second disadvantage is cost?

Jose: Only if you consider the extra money wasted. If we get the results that George wants with their knowledge of the employee handbook and we get them socialized faster as Linda wants, the extra cost may be entirely worthwhile. [Here, Kate has to make a decision. She knows that she can ferret out several more disadvantages of the small group approach. On the other hand, she senses in Jose's remark the building of a consensus. Kate doesn't want to fog the issue by putting too many pro's and con's on the table. In her judgment, the group has examined the major advantages and disadvantages, even if others could be discussed. She therefore moves the discussion on toward decision making. Vic, she notes, was the only team member left out of Jose's remarks. She attempts to include Vic now.]

Kate: Vic, do you see the extra money as well spent from a recruiting point of view?

Vic: Definitely. When I talk to job candidates, I can make a big plus out of the fact that we don't herd new people together but instead give them some individualized attention in smaller groups. That alone is worth the money.

Kate [testing now for possible consensus]:   Are we ready to move toward a decision on this? [She looks at the group and waits for verbal or nonverbal reaction from each member. They individually indicate agreement. Kate has to decide now whether to put this into her own language or to let a group member do so. She thinks, rightly, that her language version of the agreement will be easily understandable and on target. On the other hand, she knows that the team will feel more ownership of the agreement if it comes in the language of someone other than the team leader. Kate therefore turns to George.]

Kate [in a kidding tone]:   George, because lawyers are so good with words, maybe you can help frame this for us.

George: It sounds like we're agreed that the small group approach to orientation should be tried if we can resolve the issues of extra cost and the problem that the groups will be of different sizes.

Kate: Let's go around the circle for comments one way or the other before we cast anything in granite. [Kate doesn't rely on nods of the head to indicate consensus. She wants each team member to have a chance to express themselves fully on the issue.] Vic?

Vic: I think the small group approach is worth trying.

Linda: So do I.

Jose: Me too.

George: I'm in agreement, but there are those wrinkles to iron out.

Kate: Here's what I suggest. Before we invest more time and energy in the small group approach, let's check with the executive committee to see if the additional expenditure is even a possibility. If so, we can come back to this issue to resolve the question of group size. [Group indicates agreement with Kate's guidance.]

This meeting scenario has a happy ending. The executive committee agreed to the additional funding, the problem of group size was resolved by not segregating new employees according to department, and Kate's team was given high marks by corporate leaders for an innovative improvement to the orientation process. Vic and Linda did not marry, but at least work together more productively now as team members. Kate has been promoted to membership on the executive committee, in large part due to her talent as a shrewd team leader.

INSIGHT 37	Principles of team leadership are relatively easy to list, but are much more difficult to apply in the heat of discussion during a team meeting. A good team leader can *do* leadership skills, not merely describe them.

Your Turn

Pick one moment within this team meeting scenario where, in your view, Kate (the team leader) could have taken a different leadership direction with regard to members of the team. Describe that leadership alternative, explain why it has merit, and tell how you think it would have turned out for the team.

Summing Up

The minute-by-minute challenges of team leadership include careful consideration of company and team goals, member personalities, individual and group agendas, interpersonal conflict, team ownership of its ideas and decisions, the relationship of the leader to the team, recognition of team members, and many other issues that affect the processes and outcomes of the team. Wise team leaders let other team members have a hand on the wheel of the forward-moving team, but prevent any sudden moves from causing accidents or sending the team in the wrong direction.

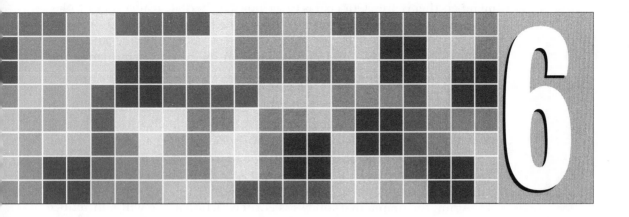

Observing Team Member Skills at Work

GOALS

- Understand that realities perceived by team members may differ significantly from realities perceived by the team leader.

- Learn to be aware of nuances and signals that other levels of team dynamics may be at work than those apparent at first glance.

- Adapt both leadership and member behaviors to allow for the reality of differing perceptions and intentions.

In the last chapter, we went along for the ride as Kate Conway led a team meeting. In this chapter, we revisit *exactly the same meeting*, at least in the words said, but observe it this time from the perspectives of the team members themselves. Our goal is to see how an alternate reality may be playing itself out within the team meeting—a reality largely ignored or misinterpreted by the team leader. We will observe how differing and often conflicting perspectives and personalities on the team can influence and often upset the results intended by the meeting leaders. In Chapter 5 we portrayed "best practices" behaviors of the team leader. In this chapter, we trace just the opposite—the underside of team politics, infighting, and cliques. Observing these "worst practices" can be extremely useful in getting team leaders and members to reflect realistically on what may be taking place beyond their intentions in team dynamics. In short, team leaders and members must recognize that people on teams don't always think, say, or do what they are supposed to from a leader's perspective.

Again, the drama that follows is entirely fictional. We will reintroduce you to team members, in case you have forgotten their personalities somewhat from the previous chapter. We will also introduce you more thoroughly to Kate Conway, the team leader.

WELCOME BACK TO THE NEW EMPLOYEE ORIENTATION TEAM

As in Chapter 5, please assume in the following scenario that five members, including team leader Kate Conway, have gathered for their second meeting to discuss how best to orient new employees to the culture, procedures, resources, and rules of the company. Here's an introduction to Kate Conway and a recap of the previous introductions of team members.

> Kate Conway, 34, came to the company as a marketing representative 4 years ago and has risen rapidly to head of the marketing department. In that time she has made her share of enemies as well as admirers in the firm. Kate's style is to do her homework, state her point forcefully, and drive home her agenda in a way that some coworkers view as relentless. Kate's promotion to head of marketing bypassed several colleagues with more seniority in the department. Although they admit her merits, they continue to feel somewhat disgruntled by her success. The company grapevine continues to portray Kate Conway as an extremely bright but overly assertive person who is easier to admire than to like. Unbeknownst to Kate, the executive committee has assigned her as team leader of the orientation team to test her abilities in working with a wide variety of personalities from several company departments. Kate's future success in the company will depend on her ability to lead teams. The executive committee has asked one team member, George, to report confidentially to them on Kate's team leadership prowess.

> A recap of other team members:

> Jose Velasquez, 40, is a mid-level personnel manager who has worked for the company for 5 years. He tends to be rather quiet during team meetings,

speaking up only when he feels he is on the majority side of any issue. Jose is a people person and does whatever he can to make others on the team feel comfortable. He becomes uncomfortable himself when team members appear to be irritated or angry with one another.

Linda Johnson, 29, is a manager in the accounting department of the company. Although she regularly takes on new employees as her subordinates, she does not understand why her boss insisted that she serve on this orientation team. She has often pointed out that she is an accountant and does not have direct expertise in personnel matters. She does have strong opinions, however, and often expresses them as final judgments rather than suggestions.

George Han, 52, is one of the company's lawyers. His primary interest lies in making sure that new employees know the rules, procedures, and guidelines contained in the employee handbook. Although he gets along well with the rest of the team, he has little patience for orientation proposals that have to do with company culture, motivation, and a welcoming entry into the employee family.

Vic Benson, 26, is a recruitment specialist who has worked for the company for only 1 year. He is a high-energy, slap-on-the-back person who seems in a perpetual rush. Vic frequently arrives late at meetings; in discussion, he tends to rush to early conclusions and decisions. He is always one of the first to speak up on any topic and often cuts others off in mid-sentence to insert his own opinions.

THE MEETING BEGINS AGAIN

Team Leader Kate: It's a few minutes after 10:00, so let's get started. Vic obviously isn't here yet, but I don't think we should wait any longer. [Members exchange glances; they know Vic's habits, but they also wonder if Kate's remark has an edge to it. Does her attitude toward Vic reflect her general attitude toward team members?] I've asked Jose to give us a quick overview of our main topic today. Jose? [Team members silently question why Kate isn't providing this overview herself. Jose was surprised when she contacted him the day before the meeting with the request that he introduce the topic at the meeting. Jose dislikes making presentations of any kind. He thought Kate knew that about him. He agrees to do what Kate asks, but resents doing so.]

Jose: Sure. The main thing we have to discuss today, and I guess make some decisions about, is whether we want the new employees—let's say 40 of them or so—to meet as a group for orientation or in smaller sets of maybe 8 or 10. Personally, I don't see where it makes that much difference because they are all going to get the same information anyway. [Jose purposely throws out his last comment as a challenge to Kate. He doesn't think the supposed main topic of the meeting is worth talking about.]

[At this point Vic bursts into the room, papers bulging from a file folder in his hand. He grabs an empty chair at the table and gives an "oops!" look to Kate and other members. Vic considers himself one of the most active contributors to the company. He works extraordinarily long hours and seldom gives himself a moment to breathe. For example, this morning he met four job applicants for interviews starting at 8:00 A.M. No wonder he was a minute or two late for this team meeting. In his list of job priorities, this team came in dead last, but as usual, he will try to contribute with energy and enthusiasm—qualities he finds missing in most of his coworkers. Because Kate says nothing about his late arrival, he assumes that she recognizes his busy schedule and will make allowances for it in the future.]

Kate: Thanks, Jose. Vic, we're discussing whether to orient new employees in a big group or smaller groups. [Vic appreciates this recognition of his presence. Kate must obviously think highly of him. She then speaks to the rest of the team.] What are your thoughts? [The team isn't used to this vague question from a team leader. Most members look down to indicate to Kate and one another that they aren't willing to bite on this bait from the leader. Vic, however, plunges in.]

Vic [eagerly]:   What do you mean by smaller groups? [Kate at this point is tempted to tell Vic, "If you had been here on time you would know we're talking about 8 to 10 people in a group." Instead, she turns over this disciplinary role to the team itself by looking to other members for a reply. For his part, Vic thinks this is the logical question. How was he supposed to know that the team had already defined the term?]

George [emphasizing how strange it was that a member began the meeting instead of the appointed leader, says pointedly to Vic]:   Jose opened the meeting by suggesting that there would be 8 to 10 people in a small group. That sounds about right to me. [Vic appears ready to talk back to George, but Kate heads him off by addressing a question to Linda from accounting. Vic looks questioningly at the rest of the team members. Is Kate going to run the whole meeting in this pushy fashion?] Linda, your department sees a lot of these new employees. What are your thoughts about the question of group size?

Linda [willing to respond even though she feels Vic has been snubbed by Kate]:   All I notice is that my new employees seem pretty isolated for the first few weeks. I'm no personnel expert, but there must be ways to make them feel part of the company more quickly. [Kate allows a pause to see if Jose will speak up. The team, however, interprets this awkward pause as a criticism of some kind for what Linda has said. Why didn't Kate say something nice to Linda? Was Kate going to allow a big pause after each person's contribution? If so, she wouldn't get much from these members.]

Vic: Well, I recruited a lot of these people and they don't have social problems, if that's what Linda is saying. They were all very friendly to me. Maybe it's just the environment in accounting. [Vic intends this as a humorous jibe at Linda, nothing more. He trusts that Linda and the rest of the team will understand his sarcasm as levity, but Kate seems to take his words literally.]

Kate [directing the team]:   Let's stick to the question of group size for a few minutes. Thoughts? [Vic winces. Why is Kate playing the heavy when he is just trying to bring a lighter moment to the meeting? This team thing was going to be a drag if Kate didn't loosen up soon. Vic notices that Kate seems to punish him by turning her attention to Jose and George.]

George: We've always done orientation in a big group and got it done in only a couple of days. I don't see any reason to make more work for ourselves. [George has joined the team in its general resistance to Kate. He, too, wants to signal that this whole discussion is going down the wrong path—one more wasted meeting on his way to retirement.]

Jose: But George, have you been satisfied with the results of that kind of orientation? I mean, are they really "oriented" from your perspective? [George and Jose have a long-standing dispute over the nature of orientation. Certainly they thought Kate knew about their history of sparring in the company. George focused on the "hard" side of orientation—policies and procedures—and accused Jose of being interested only in the "soft" side of orientation, including the socialization of new employees and activities intended to reveal company culture. Kate, however, seems somehow pleased with this opening jab by Jose. She must like conflict. The grapevine may be right about her.]

George [takes up the challenge from Jose and jabs back]:   Well, they don't know what they should about the employee handbook—

Vic [senses that the old Jose–George wars are about to resume and tries heroically to head them off with a neutral comment]:   That handbook needs a complete rewriting and— [Kate has the nerve, from Vic's point of view, to keep him from his peacemaking efforts. She cuts him off!]

Kate: Just a second, Vic. Let George finish his thought. [Vic sinks back in his chair, resigned to another battle of words between Jose and George. Was Kate actually trying to provoke this battle?]

George: I was just saying that new employees aren't very well prepared when it comes to understanding the policies and procedures of the company. [Here we go again, thinks Vic, with a discouraged look toward Linda. She too seems annoyed that Kate hasn't managed to head off this old antagonism between Jose and George.]

Jose: So maybe we can improve by putting them in smaller groups. [George shrugs his shoulders, trying to indicate to Kate and the whole team that he was absolutely fed up with Jose's typical touchy-feely approach to orientation.]

Kate: Well, let's start there. What advantages do we see in using smaller groups for orientation? [George takes this tack on Kate's part as an insult. She is obviously taking up Jose's side. Why didn't she read his shrug correctly and ask him what problems he saw with smaller groups? To George's view, Kate is definitely taking Jose's side.]

Linda: In smaller groups at least we would have a chance to get to know them individually and see if they have questions or misunderstandings. I mean, in a group of 40 it's just lecture, lecture, lecture for 2 days straight. [Linda is inclined toward Jose's point of view. She sticks it to George with her accusation of "lecture, lecture, lecture." George, after all, was one of the main speakers at last year's orientation.]

Jose [welcoming his allies and trying to consolidate his position against George]:   That's right. People do tend to speak up with their questions a lot more in small groups.

Vic [eager to concur with Linda, in whom he has growing interest]:   I think they could get to know each other easier in small groups than in one big group. [George feels outnumbered at this point. Is Kate going to steamroll over his ideas and side with his opponents? Apparently so.]

Kate: That's a good point, Vic. So the second reason has to do with socialization. That supports what you were saying, Linda— [George groans inwardly and resolves silently to quit the team or see a new leader installed.]

Linda: Right. If my new employees knew even a handful of people to have coffee or lunch with from the beginning, they would be a lot better off and probably more productive in their first few weeks. [Kate gives every sign that she likes the way the discussion has developed. George is incensed. Is the team leader totally unaware of what's really taking place? He tries a lawyer's trick by leading the discussion down a blind alley.]

George [with feigned innocence]:   I guess another advantage would be dividing people up according to which department they will be going to. If Linda's people need to get to know each other, we could put them together into one of the orientation groups. [George knows full well that new employees can't be divided into groups according to department. Some groups will be two or three times larger than other groups. George sits back to see how his ploy works out.]

Jose [senses that something is amiss and is eager to turn George's gambit back on him]:   No problem. George, should we do the same thing with new employees and interns who will be working with your people in administration?

George [forced to point out the trap he has laid for others]:   I don't see why not. Our group may be smaller than Linda's, of course. [In the heavy sarcasm of George's tone, Kate finally sniffs the conflict heating up among group members. She tries awkwardly, in George's view, to bolster Jose's position under the guise of a summary.]

Kate: So, summing up for a minute, we seem to feel that small groups would provide better orientation toward the employee handbook, let people ask questions and make comments, get to know one another, and be divided according to where they're going to work in the company. Did I get it right? [Kate waits for verbal or nonverbal approval from the team before moving ahead. George gives her no sign at all. She turns her attention to him in an effort to win complete consensus.] But George, you started to touch on a disadvantage . . .

George [with the same heavy sarcasm, which has now become obvious to everyone except Kate]:   I'm not sure if it's a disadvantage, but the groups won't all be the same size.

Vic [in another attempt at peacemaking by trying to say something supportive of George]:   Sounds like a disadvantage to me. If one group has three people in it, they will either feel they're special or that they're being singled out for some reason.

Linda [more and more willing to go along with Vic, her newfound friend]:   If I were in a group of three people and I knew others were in groups of 10 or so, I would feel persecuted. New employees always seem to see the glass as half empty instead of half full.

Kate [appearing to the group to be casting about for where to go with the discussion]:   So one disadvantage may be the different sizes of groups. Any other disadvantages? [Where are we going with this, the group wonders? Is she trying to undercut the advantages of small groups? If so, why? Whose side is she really on?]

Jose [trying to give Kate a strong hint as to how she should be proceeding]:   I'm totally in favor of the small group approach. [Kate is apparently deaf to his guidance.]

Kate: No matter how we each feel about it right now, let's do the 'due diligence' thing and at least think through any disadvantages. Jose, from a personnel point of view, do small groups pose any problem in this kind of situation? [What does she want from me, Jose wonders. I've already told her I want small groups. We have George on the ropes. Why let him have a chance to bounce back?]

Jose [trying to end discussion of the issue, speaking definitively]:   There's a ton of research on small group behaviors. The only thing I can think of could be some kind of us-against-them attitude on the part of the groups. For example, if we put Linda's people all in a group from day one, they are never going to feel part of the same team as George's new people or, for that matter, the new employees coming to work with Vic and me.

Kate [repeating Jose's point in a way that makes the group think she is simply stalling for time]:   So, I'm hearing that people may identify too much with their small group rather than the company. Any other disadvantages?

Vic [trying to move the discussion along]:   It's going to cost personnel more to run four sections of 10 people than one section of 40 people. Linda can probably estimate for us. [Vic passes the ball to Linda, who gives him an appreciative smile.]

Linda: Just a rough estimate, really. Small groups will probably cost about 50 percent more than doing orientation the old way with one big group.

George [utterly disgusted by the whole meeting]:   Now there's a disadvantage for you. [The group chuckles at his dismay and at his expense, but Kate won't let the matter rest.]

Kate: So our second disadvantage is cost?

Jose [deciding to take the high road and save the team leader from her utter confusion about where the meeting is going]:   Only if you consider the extra money wasted. If we get the results that George wants with their knowledge of the employee handbook and we get them socialized faster as Linda wants, the extra cost may be entirely worthwhile. [Jose wants to wrap this issue up before George thinks of new ways to counterattack.]

Kate: Vic, do you see the extra money as well spent from a recruiting point of view? [Jose wonders if Kate is trying to turn Vic against him. What words is she trying to put in Vic's mouth?]

Vic [always eager to boast about all he does for the company]:   Definitely. When I talk to job candidates, I can make a big plus out of the fact that we don't herd new people together but instead give them some individualized attention in smaller groups. That alone is worth the money.

Kate [to Jose's relief, as she finally begins to smell the coffee]:   Are we ready to move toward a decision on this? [She looks at the group and waits for verbal or nonverbal reaction from each member. They individually indicate agreement. George, of course, has a sneer displayed for all to see—even Kate notices that he seems to have something more he wants to say. She therefore calls on him.]

Kate [in a kidding tone that George takes as ridicule]:   George, because lawyers are so good with words, maybe you can help frame this for us. [Insult me all you wish, George thinks. Your time will come.]

George [with dripping irony and resignation]:   It sounds like we're agreed that the small group approach to orientation should be tried if we can resolve the issues of extra cost and the problem that the groups will be of different sizes.

[This last part of his comment reminds all team members that George still has an axe to grind with Jose and will no doubt find some unexpected way of winning his point.]

Kate [apparently confused by the mixed signals she is receiving]:   Let's go around the circle for comments one way or the other before we cast anything in granite. Vic?

Vic: I think the small group approach is worth trying.

Linda: So do I.

Jose: Me too.

George: I'm in agreement, but there are those wrinkles to iron out. [George puts emphasis on his last phrase and smiles wryly at his opponents on the team. He may have lost a battle, but not the war.]

Kate: Here's what I suggest. Before we invest more time and energy in the small group approach, let's check with the executive committee to see if the additional expenditure is even a possibility. If so, we can come back to this issue to resolve the question of group size.

This meeting contained exactly the same words, in the same order, as the meeting described in Chapter 5. The difference between the meetings lay entirely in the perceptions and intentions of the people involved. Which meeting actually took place? Where does reality lie?

For our purposes, the important point is this: The team meeting from Kate's point of view and the team meeting from the members' points of view *both* took place simultaneously. Kate left the room at the end of the meeting entirely satisfied with her performance as a team leader and ready to chalk up another win in her rapid rise within the company. Team members left the room equally convinced that the Jose versus George struggle had ruined one more meeting and, in the process, bamboozled the clueless team leader. From the team's perspective, the leader retreated at the end to hide behind the executive committee and their judgments.

How did things turn out in this alternative version of reality? George, an influential lawyer in the company, talked privately to his buddies on the executive committee. He told them in no uncertain terms that he wanted Kate removed as team leader. In a cynical move not unknown in corporate politics, Kate was taken out of her team leadership position by giving her a token place on the executive committee. She was promoted out of the problem George thought she helped to create. George ended up winning at least half his point: Vic, Linda, and Jose did not get to segregate their new employees into groups according to department. All new employees were simply lumped together, then divided into four equally sized groups. George was invited by the executive committee to give his standard lecture to each

group, quadrupling George's compensation from the budget of the personnel department. Jose, to George's delight, was furious at this unexpected development. He vows some form of organizational revenge at an upcoming
team meeting.

INSIGHT 38   The "true" version of an event is subject to human interpretation. Every leader
and member must have the humility and wisdom to admit that alternative realities may be taking place in the team process and, when possible, to understand and make use of them.

Your Turn

Have you encountered a team leader, professor, boss, or other group leader who seemed out
of touch with the reality of the situation as viewed by members of the team or group? If so,
write about how this individual managed to ignore or misinterpret circumstances that seemed
obvious to others. If you have not experienced this situation, you are indeed blessed. Write
about ways in which you stay in touch with what others think and feel.

Summing Up

Leaders can easily miss signs of conflict by focusing too narrowly on their
own perspectives, agendas, and feelings. Team members send important signals of their misgivings and interpersonal tensions by tone of voice, facial
expressions, lack of eye contact, sarcasm, and other means. A skilled team
leader pays attention to these expressions as indicators of the team's degree
of cohesion and synergy.

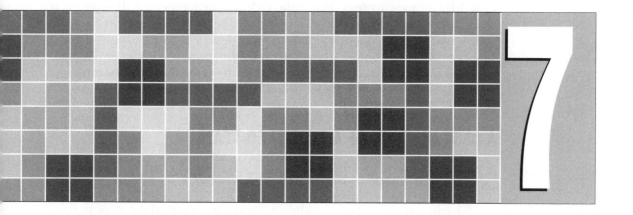

Understanding and Resolving Team Problems

GOALS

- Recognize team problems in their early stages.
- Understand the causes of such problems so they can be prevented in the future.
- Learn techniques for resolving a variety of common team problems.

Trouble in team paradise? Not all teams function smoothly and effectively in business or other organizations. Simply gathering a group of workers together and calling them a team does not guarantee they will act as a team or that the company will gain the benefits of teamwork.

Understanding the problems teams face is often difficult. When teams aren't working well, companies usually don't rush to *The Wall Street Journal* to tell their woes. Instead, they quietly bury their mistakes, dissolve their teams, and return to previous ways of organizing work. This chapter faces the reality that teams frequently encounter a variety of problems, some of them so serious that the company gives up on teams entirely. A better option, and certainly a more cost-effective one, is to understand the primary causes of team problems and assemble tools and techniques to resolve those issues.

A CASE HISTORY OF A TROUBLED TEAM

A West Coast executive tells this story of his company's experience with troubled teams:

> We followed a high-paid consultant's advice and organized our work processes around teams. Perhaps we expected too much too soon. The fact is that work flow and decision making slowed dramatically, as teams got used to working with one another and had meetings, meetings, meetings to deal with even small decisions. After about 6 weeks the company grapevine was carrying the message loud and clear: This team thing just doesn't work. We convened our executive committee to make a decision whether to struggle on with the team organization or to go back to our traditional work roles and reporting order.
>
> Before we made that decision, however, we took time to investigate what had gone wrong with our teams. We discovered three problems: We hadn't trained employees to work as team members, we hadn't revised the pay and bonus structure in the company to reward teamwork, and we hadn't realized that new ways of working would yield new kinds of results, not the same deliverables we were used to. Instead of scrapping the teams, therefore, we invested money and time in a 2-month intensive training program for all employees, top to bottom. We haven't ironed out all the wrinkles, but we're definitely seeing progress in the form of morale, innovation, and flexibility to meet changing market conditions.[1]

This corporation survived its turbulent period with teams and now continues to reap the benefits of a motivated, team-based workforce. The lesson? Don't assume that teams will run smoothly on their own. Prepare your employees for what they can expect and contribute as team members and monitor teams carefully for the first signs of trouble.

We can follow that general advice as an organizing principle for this chapter. First, we will discuss five ways in which employees can be taught to work well as team members. Second, we will investigate the 10 most common problems faced by teams across industries and organizations. Finally, for each of these problems, we will suggest techniques and tools for repairing problems and preventing their recurrence.

---

[1] Personal conversation, October 1, 2001.

A team problem is an opportunity to make the team stronger. Team members, the team leader, and upper management can all participate in that opportunity.	**INSIGHT 39**

	Your Turn
Recall a recent team experience that in some way was unsatisfactory to you. Was the problem treated as an opportunity for improvement? Explain your answer.	

TEACHING PEOPLE HOW TO BE TEAM MEMBERS

Putting several people together in the same room and giving them a common task in no way guarantees that they will work together effectively to accomplish that goal. Usually the reason has little to do with the intelligence, loyalty, or intentions of the people involved. Too often they simply don't know how to be members of a team. This may be especially true of fast-track, competitive workers who have little patience with group discussion, consensus building, and shared decision making. Even the company's brightest and best employees may have difficulty making the transition from independent contributors to team contributors.

Here, in no particular order, are five lessons that employees must learn well if they are to function effectively as members of a team.

1. Team members must know how to listen. This statement may seem like an innocuous truism comparable to "birds must know how to fly," but sometimes the most obvious truths are the most ignored. As people rise in power, recognition, and compensation within an organization, they often become so enamored of their own insights, opinions, and perspectives that they prevent others from getting a word in edgewise. You may have worked for a boss who lost his or her ears in this way. When you walked into such a boss's office, you knew in advance that you wouldn't get a chance to tell much of your story or make your point. The boss would immediately launch into a sermon that you could only bring to an end by nodding agreement.

Listening requires acknowledgment that the other person may have something worthwhile to say. Even if the content of the person's words is not particularly memorable or valuable, a good boss (or team member) listens anyway. People often communicate much between the words by their eye contact, body language, pauses, sighs, hesitations, and other meaningful signals.

One technique for practicing better listening habits is the "20 breaths" test. When the person begins talking to you about something of importance, see if you can listen to that person for 20 of your own breaths before inserting your own perspectives or objections. (You could also look at your watch, of course, and try to listen for 60 seconds. The problem here is that the person will see you glancing at the clock and draw the conclusion that you are more interested in the time than in what's being said.)

2. Team members must know how to contribute concisely. As people rise in position and importance within an organization, they often feel they have a license to bore—that is, to talk as much as they want to in meetings. They ramble on, repeat their point more than once, and ignore the stifled yawns (silent screams) of their audience. This talent for too much talk isn't exclusively reserved for managers on the rise. Lower-ranking employees, especially those who want to impress their superiors, also can hold forth much longer than anyone wishes. This unfortunate behavior can be death to a team environment. No one wants to be stuck with one or more "big talkers" for the weeks or months that a team may be active.

The answer to this dilemma is not to shut people up—a poor practice on any team—but to remind people to get to the point (once, thank you).

3. Team members must understand the nature of team discussion and decision making. We each have different tolerance and expectation levels for group discussion. Some of us get antsy if an issue can't be presented, discussed, and resolved within a matter of minutes. Others, perhaps those who like committee work, seem content to let discussion meander for hours without any sign of resolution. These differences in discussion habits can rip a team apart. All team members have to have approximately the same model in mind for how—and how long—a topic is discussed; how consensus is achieved or at least attempted; and how group decisions are made without creating winners and losers on the team. These skills and group experiences are a matter of training. Lacking such development, workers will probably persist in their individual approaches to discussion, sure that everyone else on the team is doing it wrong.

4. Team members must know how to criticize ideas without criticizing personalities. "I think you're wrong" is the kind of phrase that sets tempers on edge among team members. "I don't agree with your point" changes the focus to the idea at hand rather than the person espousing the idea. Again, a short training session can make all workers aware of this simple but crucial adjustment in thinking and perspective.

5. Team members must be able to rely on others for help. "Lone rangers" are alive and well in companies and other organizations. These are the rugged individualists—corporate survivalists, really—who depend only on themselves to fulfill all aspects of their job responsibilities. Although these people may make productive employees in some work environments, they make lousy team members. Just as children learn early on to play together

and share toys, so team members must be socialized at some point (obviously in a more sophisticated way) to work together and share resources.

The knowledge and skills required to be an effective team member do not come naturally to most people. We learn to become team members just as we learn many other professional roles.	**INSIGHT 40**

Your Turn
Based on your team experience, which of the five training suggestions in this section seems most important to you? Explain why.

FIVE COMMON TEAM PROBLEMS AND TOOLS FOR REPAIR AND PREVENTION

Now that we have prepped our potential team members by training them to listen, contribute concisely, discuss patiently, criticize objectively, and rely on one another, we can set the team in motion and see how it spins. If we observe a wobble or worse, the fault probably lies in one of the following five team maladies:

Unsuitable Personalities

Not everyone is cut out to be a team member, even with prior training. If most team members agree that one or two individuals are causing the team to founder, investigate their opinion and act promptly to deal with (probably remove) the problematic individual. (We aren't talking here about the individual whose opinions differ from those of the majority on the team; this person can be valuable as a devil's advocate or the "loyal opposition." A problematic team member is one whose character or personality subverts the trust level and basic processes shared by other team members.)

The Fink

This individual offends other team members by "talking out of school"—that is, gossiping to outsiders about privileged discussion among team members. In unguarded discussion, all team members occasionally say something that they would not like quoted to certain other individuals, perhaps a boss, outside the team. To have their words shared and often distorted without their consent is an intolerable rift in the trust level that team members must assume for frank discussion.

Inveterate finks must be removed from teams. Accidental finks (those who are trying out fink behavior for the first time) can be saved for team service by having their behavior called to their attention, preferably by the boss. "If I want to know what Alice thinks," a boss can say to the wanna-be fink, "I will ask Alice. Don't start harmful rumors." That kind of frank response usually alerts a fink to his or her objectionable behavior.

INSIGHT 41	"Talking out of school" as a team member ends up hurting both the team and the person spreading rumors about the team.

Your Turn	
How do you respond when someone approaches you with hot news about an otherwise confidential matter at work?	

The Stone

This is the individual who rarely speaks up in team discussion, seldom volunteers for responsibility, and seems to have no opinion when it comes to decision making. The silence of the Stone can arise from basic shyness (not uncommon for new employees), annoyance at being put on the team, plain laziness, or other causes.

Discover what's going on inside the Stone by means of an individual, heart-to-heart conference. If the cause of this individual's silence is shyness, work with other team members in making the individual feel more a part of the group. If the individual dislikes serving on the team, find something else for this person to do. No team should have to endure an unwilling member. If the Stone is simply kicking back and letting others do the work, give the individual a significant work assignment and make its accomplishment part of the person's performance evaluation.

The Objector

An objection can no doubt be raised to any statement uttered by a human being. Do you object? The problem with the Objector is that this person has no other discussion technique beyond objection. Sometimes the Objector has developed this discussion habit as a way of attracting attention, albeit largely negative attention, or the Objector may simply have a speculative mind that needs exercise by playing the pros and cons game with every imaginable assertion.

Within moderation, Objectors serve a valuable function for the team by preventing GroupThink and other rushes to team judgment, but when this individual puts up roadblocks to team discussion at every opportunity, something must be done. Perhaps the team itself can have a discussion with the Objector (if he or she doesn't object!) in an effort to understand the person's one-track approach, or the team leader can privately make the Objector aware of how this behavior undercuts the work of the team.

The Petty Tyrant

This individual is a verbal bully. Through sarcasm, ridicule, temper tantrums, and other emotional displays, the Petty Tyrant makes his or her mood the real agenda for every team meeting. Discussion is held captive by this person's interpersonal aggression. As a general rule, the personality defects that allow a Petty Tyrant to behave in this way are not amenable to quick fixes by a chat with the team leader or intervention by the team itself (although both approaches are always worth a try). It's often necessary to remove the Petty Tyrant, but seldom necessary to apologize to the team for doing so.

Silence, constant objection, and tyrannous domination of others are behaviors that make teamwork impossible.	**INSIGHT 42**

Your Turn
Call to mind someone from your experience with teams who fits one of the previous descriptions. How did the team respond to this individual? How did you respond? What finally happened?

The Word Machine

Jerry Seinfeld's famous phrase, "yada yada yada," typifies the Word Machine. The Word Machine manages to turn a simple thought into a long harangue through three verbal devices. First, the Word Machine creates a series of paraphrases for the same idea: "I went to lunch because it was noon and I needed to eat, which is pretty much what I do every day around 12 o'clock, because we get an hour or so off work at that time for, you know, the midday meal." Second, the Word Machine tells not only what things are but what they aren't: "I stapled the pages together. I didn't use a paperclip or tape or a manila folder or those spiral bindings you can get at the copy shops." Finally, the Word Machine accompanies every expression of thought with a record of personal information or emotion: "I got here at 8:00 A.M., even though I'm not really a morning person, probably because I had to get up early with my kids for all those years and I finally said to myself, 'Enough of this greet-the-dawn routine,' so now I just work out some kind of flextime so that usually I don't have to get here early, like I did this morning."

The Word Machine doesn't mean to be annoying. In most cases, he or she simply likes to chatter and assumes (against all nonverbal evidence) that others don't mind listening. Intentions aside, the Word Machine can be dangerous to team processes if other team members begin to dread meetings; if a significant percentage of valuable team time is taken up by such gabble; or if the team fails to discuss topics thoroughly because of constant distractions from the Word Machine.

Talking to the Word Machine seems somehow redundant, akin to carrying water to the lake. Because a good shaking is out of professional bounds, the team leader can meet privately with the Word Machine and say something along these lines: "You're a very nice person and we all like you. Do you realize that you talk much, much more than any other team member? You've got to let others have their fair share of our discussion time." As an alternative to this conversation, a team leader can make a copy of the Word Machine discussion in this book and leave it in the Word Hog's office mail.

INSIGHT 43	Saying too much too often is as ruinous to team proceedings as failing to contribute at all.

Your Turn	
Certainly you have worked with someone who simply talks too much. Why do you think this person is so talkative? How can this tendency be controlled?	

The Stalled Team

Even the most promising of teams have times when work bogs down and progress comes to a halt. The causes of such unexpected stalls usually can be determined only by a careful review of the business circumstances and team processes existing at the time. In general, however, teams experience periods of frustrating stagnation for one or more of the following reasons.

1. Team members are exhausted from an overly ambitious work schedule. Their inability to press on with work is a way of telling people in the company that they need a break of some kind.

2. Team members have experienced some kind of disappointment or dead end. Perhaps one of their decisions, for example, has been soundly rejected by upper management. In this case, the stall they are experiencing stems from a lack of motivation to press ahead with work that apparently is not respected or approved in the organization.

3. Team members have a problem of some kind with the team leader. Members sometimes "go to ground" in not-so-subtle protest against what they perceive as overly dominant leadership, favoritism on the part of the leader, or perhaps too little leadership.

4. Team members have a problem with one another. The stall reflects their common judgment that team processes have broken down.

TOOLS FOR REPAIR

Like a stalled car, a stalled team can either be jump-started by an outside energy source of some kind or turned on again by repair of its own internal workings. If the new start comes from an outside source, it is usually in the form of a meeting with one or more senior managers who are not part of the team but are nonetheless responsible for its progress. At this meeting (or series of meetings) the senior manager expresses confidence in the team, reviews their positive accomplishments in the past, and investigates through active listening and probing questions, the circumstances (as team members perceive them) causing the current stall. The senior manager leads the team to a solution that, preferably, the team itself helps to shape. An imposed solution usually has less power to restart a team; participative buy-in to the solution is a critical component of a workable answer to the team's problems.

If the jump start comes from within the team itself, it can take the form of a retreat of some kind, in which the team gets away from its usual surroundings and work issues to approach its problems in a fresh way. Some teams arrange an off-site day at a resort location or other meeting place where natural beauty, creature comforts, and the opportunity to relax combine to renew team creativity and the willingness to seek solutions. At such a retreat the team leader can ask each team member to talk about what's going right and what's going wrong on the team. Discussion should move toward consensus and then toward a team-generated action plan.

A stall should not be taken as a permanent condition of the team. Stalls can be overcome by external or internal measures.   **INSIGHT 44**

Your Turn

Recall a time when a team on which you were a member reached a stall or dead end of some kind. Did the team recover? If so, how?

The Out-of-Control Team

This is the team that exceeds its envelope of authority and begins using resources and making decisions in areas where it has no business operating. Some teams make this mistake because their original charter was never made clear by management. Other teams grow power hungry within the company and attempt to gobble up other job categories and budgets that can add to their influence in the organization.

TOOLS FOR REPAIR

No matter what the cause, the runaway team must be called back into check without deflating the high energy level and motivation that characterizes the team. A senior manager can meet with the team leader to reinforce the boundaries of the team's authority and responsibility. The team leader is then given the chance to communicate these limits persuasively to members of the team. If that communication fails, the senior manager must step in again, this time in a meeting with the entire team. The senior manager can praise the team for its gung-ho spirit, but also insist that those energies be focused on the specific work assignments given to the team. Members of the team should leave that meeting feeling appreciated for the effort and reeducated about the scope of their work.

INSIGHT 45	Because they are usually composed of talented, influential individuals, teams have implicit power within organizations. When they misuse that power and exceed their authority, teams become an organizational liability.

Your Turn	
If you have observed or served on a runaway team, briefly tell its story and outcome. If you have never observed or served in this way, tell what you would do as a team member if your team showed signs of becoming a runaway group.	

The Bickering Team

No senior manager likes to have to deal with a whining, backbiting group of individuals whose single interest seems to be "who did what to whom" on the team. The bickering team, like squabbling children, seems to cry out for parenting, and yet when a senior manager steps in, he or she is immediately accused of listening to only one side of the story or taking sides unfairly. Before senior managers enter the fray, therefore, they should get the team to distill the nature of its problems. If the team itself can define the root causes of its bickering, a senior manager can usually guide the team to find its own solutions.

TOOLS FOR REPAIR

If the team can't diagnose its own ills successfully, a senior manager should meet privately with each member of the team. After hearing each person's gripes (often an unpleasant series of interviews), the manager will have a rather clear picture of what's going wrong in the team. Solutions can include reassigning certain team members, changing the leadership of the team to a person all members can accept, or exerting disciplinary authority by telling team members to act professionally if they hope to be rewarded professionally in the organization.

People squabble for hundreds of reasons. No matter what the cause, their interpersonal friction can seriously interrupt the work of teams.	**INSIGHT 46**

Your Turn
Call to mind two people who didn't get along at work. What was the source of their antipathy? Was the matter ever resolved? If so, how?

The Leaderless Team

In some companies, a stigma attaches to people who stick their necks out in taking over leadership responsibilities. As the Japanese saying goes, "The protruding nail must be hammered down." Democratic culture can be so influential in these organizations that teams attempt to do without a leader entirely. A senior manager often discovers this situation in trying to determine how the team is progressing. When the manager contacts one team member, the manager is passed along to another member with the explanation, "Well, I can only speak for my own activities on the team." The truth soon emerges that no one speaks for the team as a whole, nor does anyone know quite what the team has done, is doing, or will do.

TOOLS FOR REPAIR

A senior manager may be sorely tempted to simply appoint one member of the team as leader, in effect saying to the members, "Look, just do what Ruth tells you to do." This solution, of course, is only the beginning of bigger troubles for the team. The senior manager's designation of Ruth as leader is the kiss of death to her authority in the team. She quickly becomes the last person team members will listen to or follow. A better solution lies in working with the team so that it chooses its own leader and participates, with the senior manager's input, in defining the roles the leader will play on the team. Finally, if the spirit of individual rights is so strong on the team that no leader can be agreed on, the senior manager may have to join the team and impose a reasonable degree of leadership. This option is quite literally a case of "if you can't beat them, join them."

INSIGHT 47	Too little leadership can be as devastating to business processes as too much leadership.

Your Turn	

Tell about a time when you wanted more leadership from some individual in your business or academic life. Why do you think that person did not lead in the way you wished? How did the situation finally turn out?

HOW PEOPLE INDICATE THAT A TEAM IS IN TROUBLE

Indications that a team is in trouble frequently are not spelled out for a manager or for the team members themselves. The SOS message comes in more subtle ways. Team leaders, team members, and upper managers can watch for 10 symptoms of the troubled team:

- The work product is shoddy and deadlines are continually missed.
- Members miss meetings using suspicious excuses.
- Members treat a minor achievement as if it were the culmination of their entire work. They reveal their lack of interest in accomplishing the true goals of the team by celebrating victory too soon.
- Members gossip about and talk down their fellow team members to outsiders.
- Individual members seem to be cutting their own deals, advancing their personal agendas, and setting their own goals without regard for what the team as a whole should be doing.
- The team leader appears constantly involved with putting out small fires of controversy among team members or, just as bad, trying to hide the squabbles on the team from outside view at any cost.

- Members complain that they were under duress of some kind and were compelled by social pressure or implied threats to go along with the will of the majority.

- Particular members keep asking for individual praise for their work on the team and refuse to find any satisfaction in recognition for the entire team.

- Some members withdraw and sit sulking on the sidelines of the action taking place in the team.

- One or more members constantly play the "blame game" by attributing any team failure, however small, to ineptness on the part of the leader or other team members.

These signs, singly or in any combination, tell a good manager that trouble is brewing on the team. Early intervention can prevent major blowups, including terminations, resignations, and even lawsuits.

People do not sit idly by while the team ship begins to sink. They let outsiders know about team troubles by their words, actions, and nonverbal communications.	**INSIGHT 48**

Your Turn
If you have served on an ineffective team, tell specific ways in which you or other team members let others know about what was wrong with the team. If you have never served on an ineffective team (lucky you!), tell about signs or signals you have observed from others who did serve on such teams.

A LIGHTER LOOK AT THE CHALLENGE OF MANAGING A TEAM

Sometimes the fault with a team lies not with the team itself, but with the management style (or lack of style) of the senior manager responsible for the team. *Today's Team Facilitator* magazine takes a tongue-in-cheek swipe at managers who are themselves the source of the team problems about which they complain.[2]

---

[2] Cited in Skopec, E. *How to Use Team Building to Foster Innovation.* Chicago: NTC, 1998, p. 97.

If you want to make sure your team fails, the article proposes, simply do the following:

- Don't listen to any new idea or recommendation from a team. It's probably not a good idea because it's new and different.

- Don't give teams any additional resources to help solve their problems in their area. Teams are supposed to save money and make do with less. Besides, they probably will just waste more time and money.

- Treat all problems as signs of failure and treat all failures as reasons to disband the team and downgrade team members. Teams are supposed to make things better, not cause you more problems.

- Create a system that requires lots of reviews and signatures to get approval for all changes, purchases, and new procedures. You can't be too careful these days.

- Get the security department involved to make it difficult for teams to get information about the business. Don't let those team members near company databases. You don't want them finding out how the business is really run.

- Assign a manager to keep an eye on the teams in your area. Tell each member that he or she is there to help facilitate (teams like that word). But what you really want these managers to do is control the direction of the teams and report back to you on any deviations from your plan.

- When you recognize or change policies and procedures, don't involve team members in the decision or give them any advance warning. This will just slow things down and make it difficult to implement the changes.

- Cut out all training. Problem solving is just common sense anyway, and besides, all that training really accomplishes is to make a few consultants rich.

- Express your criticism freely and withhold praise and recognition. People need to know where they have screwed up so they can change. If you dole out praise, people will expect a raise or reward.

Again, this is all satiric advice—the precise opposite of what a good team manager should do.

| **INSIGHT 49** | The way teams are managed has much to do with the way they look upon themselves and the success with which they function. |

Your Turn

Call to mind a team on which you served. To whom did the team report? Describe how this person managed (or mismanaged) the team.

Summing Up

The fact that teams experience problems from time to time does not mean that the team concept itself is a failure or that particular teams are doomed. The first signs of such problems gives team members, the team leader, and senior management an opportunity to discover the causes of the difficulty and resolve it in a way that strengthens the team for increased productivity.

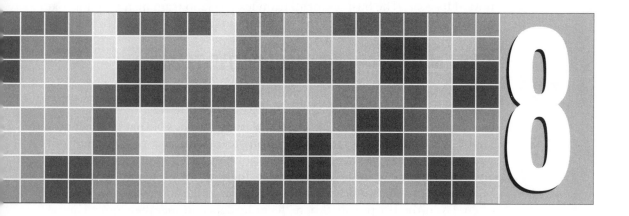

Motivating Team Members and Leaders

GOALS

- Grasp principles of motivation applicable to teams.

- Devise practical techniques for motivating high-performance behaviors for team members and leaders.

- Create motivational strategies that fit particular teams and circumstances.

"My team doesn't need motivation," one team leader boasts. "They have a lot of energy and commitment without any pushing from me." This team leader misunderstands the nature of motivation. It is not something extra that must be added if a team starts to slow down. Instead, it is the essential fuel that got the team up and running in the first place and keeps it moving toward its goals. The business of all team leaders (and team members, for that matter) should be to discover the various motivators that power their teams.

EIGHT MOTIVATORS FOR PRODUCTIVE TEAMS

Because worker motivation directly affects the bottom-line profits of virtually all companies, it has been studied in a scientific way for more than a century. This chapter sums up the 10 primary findings of that research and applies them in a way that can help your team gain or regain momentum and drive. For reasons that have to do with their backgrounds, personalities, and circumstances, individuals are influenced by different motivators. We cannot create a priority list, therefore, of which motivators work most often. From the list provided here, team leaders and members must choose the approaches that fit best for the individuals on their teams—and for themselves.

Motivation by Money

One urban myth about business suggests that money is the only motivator for work performance. Not so. In fact, in recent surveys of worker attitudes, money (compensation) ranked 5 from the top in the list of 10 motivators. (The top motivator, to satisfy your curiosity, was appreciation for their work.)

Although money doesn't deserve its entire reputation as a motivator, it nevertheless is a potent force for many team members. For example, an individual who resists joining a team may be motivated to do so by the boss's offer of a 10 percent raise, but once on the team, does that 10 percent raise continue to motivate the person's work? Probably not. Therein lies the problem with money motivation: It provides a short-term push but often fails in the longer term. The promise of money at some future date addresses this longer term problem to some degree. The boss could have told the individual, "Look, if you serve and serve well on this team, I'll raise your pay 10 percent when the team finishes its work." In this case, the worker is motivated as much by expectation as by the reality of money; in other words, his hopes and dreams for what he will do with extra cash keep him laboring away conscientiously on the team.

Or do they? Picture yourself in this person's situation. You know that you will receive, let's say, an annual raise of $6,000 if you serve well on the team. That promised compensation may well motivate you to come to team meetings, but does it motivate you minute by minute in your work with other team members? Are you thinking to yourself, "I hate what I'm doing, but I'm going to do a really good job because I'll get that $6,000"? Probably not. Even in its promised form, money has only limited power to motivate initiative, creativity, cooperation, and a gung-ho spirit on the part of team members and leaders.

The added problem with money is that most team leaders are not authorized to give it to their members. Matters of compensation are usually handled by upper management on a one-to-one basis with individual workers. The team leader is hardly ever in a position to say, "I have a large budget that I will dole out to each of you depending on your effort each week for the team."

Given these quite real problems with money as a motivator, team leaders must look beyond compensation as a primary motivator for their people and themselves. One productive way to begin that search is to ask the personal question, "What motivates me right now in the work I'm doing? Why am I trying to do it well and finish it on time?" The answers to that question may well appear in the remaining list of nonfinancial motivators.

Money should not be over-rated as a motivator of performance. It consistently ranks far from the top when workers across industries list the motivators that matter most to them on the job.	**INSIGHT 50**

Your Turn
Describe a time when money was not your primary motivation for doing a good job. What other motivators were present?

Motivation by Social Needs

The philosopher-psychologist Abraham Maslow suggested that we each must satisfy certain levels of need before we are able or interested in moving on to a higher level of need fulfillment.[1] At base, Maslow says, we satisfy our physiological needs: we get enough to eat, a place to sleep, and so on. After that we make sure we're safe. Our security needs taken care of, we are able to move on to higher needs.

Here's where Maslow's Hierarchy begins to yield interesting insights for team leaders and members. Most employees come to the workplace, after all, having satisfied their physiological and security needs. They are not starving nor do they feel imperiled. In short, they come to work ready to be motivated by higher-level needs. The next step for such workers is the need for social involvement and satisfaction.

---

[1] Maslow, Abraham H. *Motivation and Personality*. 2d ed. New York: Harper, 1970.

That need is used to this day to motivate (through negative reinforcement) the behavior of an obstreperous child at school. The child is isolated in a corner or made to stay in the empty classroom during recess. The absence of social contact can provide a strong motive for children to reform their behavior. In the workplace, such negative use of social need is rare. We don't banish people to their cubicles as a punitive measure; most would simply quit if we did so. Instead, we tend to use social needs as a positive inducement to high performance. Joining a team, for example, can be viewed as satisfying a social need: The individual is now an accepted member of a group. A certain amount of fun, personal sharing, and chat takes place on the team, all of which proves enjoyable for the person and motivates loyalty to the team and hard work on its behalf. There's a degree of protection in being part of the group, which defends its own against outside attacks.

Team leaders and members can use social needs as a strong motivator by keeping team membership highly desirable in the organization, making team activities as interesting and intellectually challenging as possible, portraying team goals as important to the organization, and purposely mixing social enjoyment of one another's company with the work agenda.

| **INSIGHT 51** | Being in the company of people you enjoy can be a motivating force in itself. You tend to give your best effort so as not to let the team down. |

| **Your Turn** | |
| Call to mind a team on which you now serve or have served. Tell any ways in which the social aspects of the team helped to motivate your work. | |

Motivation by Self-Image

We each have an image of ourselves in the workplace. One person may see himself as the bright, hard-working, and unappreciated type. Another person may view herself as a socially conscious, caring work colleague. Yet another person may have a negative self-image, thinking of himself as a person who slides by, doing as little as possible to keep from getting fired.

An image can be viewed as a standard we set for ourselves. It accompanies us from job to job, company to company, and changes as we mature through a variety of life and work experiences. Those selected as team members usually have positive self-images—they expect much from themselves and always have. The presence of this high individual standard can be used to motivate the person. "You obviously have great analytical abilities and a gift for seeing the big picture," a team leader may say. "We're depending on you to use those abilities to the fullest on our team."

Think for a moment what motivates this individual to give his or her best. Certainly it isn't the promise of compensation or the threat of being fired or the social life enjoyed by the team. The essential motivator is the person's internal commitment not to let himself or herself down—in other words, not to be less than his or her self-image. This motivation can be interpreted as fear of failing in the eyes of others: "They won't think I'm as talented as I hold myself out to be." But even removing others from the scene, the motivation is still present and powerful: "I don't want to disappoint myself."

Team leaders and members can use motivation by self-image by making much of the individual stars on the team. Frequent reference can be made to individual members' areas of expertise and past achievements. By getting people to think highly of themselves, you can motivate them to do their best work.

What we believe to be true about ourselves can motivate our performance. We don't want to appear less than we are in the eyes of others or in our own eyes.	**INSIGHT 52**

	Your Turn
List three qualities that are "you," no matter what job you find yourself in. How would you feel if you compromised or ignored these qualities in a work experience?	

Motivation by Expectancy

Part of the excitement of living and working is "the chase"—what's around the corner, what's in store tomorrow, what we will be doing 1 year from now or 5 years from now. It's human nature to imagine that future as somewhat brighter than the present. For example, we picture ourselves progressing, not regressing, in our careers. We think of ourselves as getting smarter each day, or at least getting a better sense of how the world works.

Here's the key question for motivation by expectancy: How much are we willing to do in expectation of getting something we want? If a kid—Jake—sells candy bars door-to-door in expectation of eventually receiving a new bicycle, how much goal-directed activity (selling candy bars) will he perform to get to his goal-fulfillment activities (riding his new bike)? What are the factors that influence this balance?

Victor Vroom, the American guru of expectancy motivation, proposed a three-part formula for determining the intensity of expectancy motivation:[2]

1. If you believe that your effort affects your performance
   (and)
2. If you believe that performance determines predictable outcomes
   (and)
3. If you believe that you value those outcomes . . . then you will be motivated to expend maximum or near maximum effort to achieve your goals.

Let's try this formula out in the case of Jake and his candy bars. First, does Jake believe that his hard work in going door to door affects the number of candy bars he sells? Absolutely. Second, does Jake believe that the number of candy bars sold will determine whether or not he gets his bike? Again, absolutely. Finally, does Jake really want the new bike? Yes, in spades. We can expect Jake, therefore, to be extremely motivated in his efforts to sell candy bars.

However, subtract any one of Vroom's three factors and notice how Jake's motivation sags. Let's say that Jake believes it's totally a matter of luck, not work, that determines how many candy bars are sold. His friend Jimmy got one order out of the blue for 200 bars. In this case, Jake probably won't be motivated to keep up his steady door-to-door efforts. Let's say the candy bar company is vague about exactly how many candy bar sales it takes to win the bicycle. "Just do your best, kids, and one of you will win this new bike!" When the link between performance and outcome is disturbed or broken, motivation falls apart. Jake is not going to work as hard if he is unsure whether his work will pay off.

Finally, let's tweak the third element in Vroom's formula to see how Jake's motivation is affected. Imagine that Jake, a 15-year-old, is in that betwixt-and-between age where bicycles are being left behind in favor of motorcycles. If Jake doesn't value the outcome of his work ("Do I really want a bike that much?") he will not be motivated to expend maximum effort to achieve it.

For team leaders and members, expectancy motivation has great usefulness—if it is well understood and carefully applied. Simply promising the team some "blue sky" reward for their work is not, in itself, expectancy motivation. To make any future reward potent as a motivator, the individuals on the team must believe that they can get there through effort, believe that you won't "move the cheese" as they get close to it, and believe that they

---

[2] Vroom, Victor H. *Work and Motivation.* New York: Wiley, 1964.

sincerely want the reward dangled in front of them. Lacking any of these elements, the team will not be motivated to expend significant effort.

What we expect in the future influences our performance in the present.	**INSIGHT 53**

	Your Turn

Describe your specific expectations in the future of some work-related or academic experience in which you are now involved. What part does expectancy motivation play in the effort you now give to that experience?

Motivation by Equity

"I'll do my fair share, not a bit less or more." That sentiment is widely heard within teams and expresses the equity approach to motivation. Simply stated, team leaders and members don't want to carry more than their fair share of the work. If they do carry more of the workload, they want to be rewarded more than the person who carries less of the workload. Stated as an equation, the equity theory of motivation appears thus:

$$\frac{\text{my reward}}{\text{my input}} \quad \text{should equal} \quad \frac{\text{your reward}}{\text{your input}}$$

This motivator works well for teams if their tasks are relatively discrete and can be distributed to individual team members. For example, an investigative team looking at 20 suspects can divide the workload evenly and reward each member of the team to the same degree. However, if team member A had to investigate 10 suspects and team members B, C, D, and E had only 2 or 3 each, the question of fairness (and implied motivation) would definitely arise. Person A would no doubt claim that he deserved compensation or other reward equal to the entire work of persons B, C, D, and E. His input, in other words, equaled their combined input. If person A did not receive such compensation or reward, his motivation to perform would slip considerably.

The equity approach to motivation does not work as well on teams where the workload cannot be neatly divided into same-sized bundles for distribution to team members. For example, when a creative team at an advertising agency meets to come up with a new promotional campaign, all workers seem to be doing everything all at once. There is no neat task division or comparability based on workload. Being there to participate in the work of the team becomes the primary criteria by which one's input is measured. If person A attended only half the team's meetings while persons B, C, D, and E attended all of the meetings, person A could hardly claim the same rewards as the other workers.

Team leaders and members can use equity motivation by making sure that the workload is evenly distributed among team members or, if imbalances occur, that those who do the most work receive additional rewards of some kind. Otherwise, according to equity principles, the motivation of the overworked, underrewarded individuals will begin to suffer.

INSIGHT 54   The belief that we are being treated fairly in comparison to others in our same situation is crucial to our level of motivation.

Your Turn

Call to mind a time when you believed you were treated unfairly in a work or school situation. How did your belief influence your motivation to perform in that situation?

Motivation by Appreciation

From our earliest years we are taught to think of performance as a route to approval. We clean up our toys and receive praise and a hug from a parent. (Or, in the negative version, we fail to clean up our toys and receive a stern word or worse from a parent.) As we grow up, we learn to reward ourselves for achievements and depend less on other people's evaluations, judgments, and praise, but few of us completely leave behind our need for appreciation, praise, respect, and regard from others we admire. Throughout the last two decades, Paul Hersey and Ken Blanchard have surveyed workers across industries to determine what motivates them. "Appreciation for work done" consistently came in as the number one motivator, with "feeling in on things" in second place.[3]

Appreciation does not work as a motivator, however, if the person giving the appreciation is not respected by the workers. A hated boss, for example, can express appreciation from dawn to dusk without any motivational effect if the workers put no stock in his words. In a team environment, therefore, appreciation motivates performance only when it comes from

---

[3] Hersey, Paul et al. *Management of Organizational Behavior.* Upper Saddle River, NJ: Prentice Hall, 1988.

someone the team members admire and respect. This person may be an executive or manager outside the team or may be the team leader. Appreciation from member to member on the team can also be motivating as long as those members have high regard for one another.

The range of activities and achievements for which team leaders and members can be appreciated is long indeed. Here's a sample:

- "Thanks for your hard work."
- "I appreciated your assistance with my chart."
- "Thank you for not giving up on this project."
- "I admired the way you handled conflict on the team."
- "You made the difference between success and failure on this task."
- "We all learned a lot from working with you."

Expressions of appreciation from admired people in our work lives significantly influence our motivation to give our best effort to the tasks at hand.	**INSIGHT 55**

Your Turn
We all want appreciation from some people who seem to give it too rarely. Describe a situation in which you desire an expression of appreciation from someone. If that appreciation was given, how would your motivation or attitude be influenced?

Motivation by Theory Y Principles

Douglas McGregor described two very different sets of assumptions about workers, including those who serve on teams.[4] The old-fashioned approach, McGregor asserts, can be called Theory X principles. In this view, a team leader looks out at her members and assumes

- These people all hate to work.
- No one except me is willing to accept responsibility.
- No one except me has any ambition.
- These people expect to be led.
- These people expect me to solve their problems for them.

---

[4] McGregor, Douglas. *The Human Side of Enterprise.* 5th ed. New York: McGraw Hill, 1988.

- These people come to work just for the paycheck and have no ambition for promotion.
- I'll have to watch these people closely to keep them from loafing and doing poor quality work.

Those attitudes, if proven true about the workforce, make the job of the leader difficult indeed. Who wants to come to work each day as the slave driver? Worse, who wants to come to work each day as the slave?

More modern organizations, says McGregor, have taken on new attitudes toward work and workers. These attitudes are Theory Y assumptions. In this view, a team leader looks out at her members and assumes

- Work can be pleasurable.
- Most people want reasonable levels of responsibility.
- Most people have strong goals for themselves.
- Most people like to lead occasionally.
- Most people have good problem-solving skills.
- Most people are motivated by more than money.
- Most people will give good effort to their job even when they are not being watched or prodded.

If a team leader believes this about members—and they, in turn, believe it about themselves—work life becomes much more pleasant and productive. People are motivated to give their best because they are enjoying what they are doing. Team leaders don't have to prod workers with the stick of discipline and threats because workers are already doing all the right things by themselves. The team leader is then free to encourage, shape, and guide the efforts of the team.

One way to gain the full benefit of Theory Y principles on a team is to make them more than unspoken assumptions. The team leader, for example, can express his or her confidence in team members and, using the language of Theory Y principles, let team members know that they are trusted to solve problems, take on responsibility, and share leadership. Team members can express the same thoughts to one another: "Let's figure out a way to solve this" rather than "Let's turn this over to the team leader" and "We can finish this project on time if we stay late tonight, then work only a half day tomorrow" rather than "It's 4:59 P.M. and I'm going home, even if the project is late."

| INSIGHT 56 | Thinking the worst of workers leads to poor performance on their part. Thinking the best of workers leads to superior performance. |

Motivation by the Hawthorne Effect

The story of the Hawthorne Effect[5] has been told and retold so often that it has risen to the status of a motivation parable for team leaders and members. In the 1920s, some early workplace researchers wanted to determine the influence of external factors on work productivity. They focused on a group of wiring assemblers working at the Western Electric Company in Hawthorne, Illinois. What effect does lighting have on productivity, they asked. To answer that question, they selected one group as their test sample and one group as a control sample. First, they gradually increased the illumination in the workroom of the test group (lighting was left unchanged in the control room throughout the experiments). To no one's surprise, productivity rose for the test group, but to their great surprise, productivity also rose for the control group.

These unusual results attracted the attention of Harvard's Elton Mayo. Over a period of 2 years, Mayo and his team tried all manner of workplace enhancements on the test group—rest breaks, company-paid lunches, more comfortable workstations, and so forth. To their astonishment, the control group without these favors performed as well or better than the test group. Finally, researchers took away all work enhancements from the test group and plunged these workers back to their original work conditions. Surely, researchers thought, we will now see productivity plunge as workers react negatively to these changes. Just the opposite occurred. Production for the test group reached an all-time high.

From this famous experiment came the notion of the Hawthorne Effect: Any group singled out for special attention, even for control purposes, will usually respond with increased motivation. Simply being put in the spotlight as special gives people and teams a boost of energy to perform. Mayo and his team had located a central truth of motivation: More than in any external circumstances such as lighting, motivation for performance resides within human beings. People make the difference in organizations. How they are treated makes the difference in their performance.

---

[5] The story of Elton Mayo's research and the "Hawthorne Effect" is told in Smith, D. M., *Motivating People.* New York: Barron's, 1997, p. 41ff.

Team leaders and members can use the Hawthorne Effect by making the most of the unique nature of the team in the organization, the visibility and importance of its work, and the special regard in which the team is held by the organization. This spotlight of respect becomes a self-fulfilling prophecy. Teams perform up to the special standards attributed to them.

INSIGHT 57	Being considered special in some way motivates us to perform up to the level of that reputation or recognition.

Your Turn

Describe a time when your team or you as an individual were highlighted in some way for your special status, abilities, or other attributes. How did this spotlight of attention influence your motivation to perform?

Summing Up

Every team leader and team member must pay attention not only to ways in which others are motivated, but also to ways that motivate them as individuals. Among the eight key motivators for teams are motivation by money, social needs, self-image, expectancy, equity, appreciation, Theory Y principles, and the Hawthorne Effect. Teams can use a variety of these approaches to keep members eager to do their best work and committed to achieving the goals of the team and the organization.

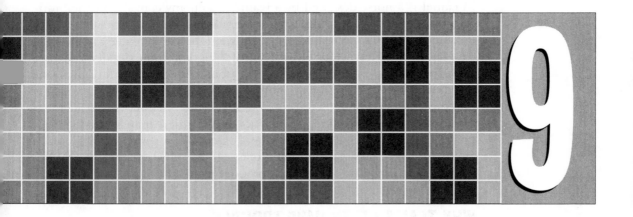

Completing Collaborative Projects Through Teamwork

GOALS

- Understand common obstacles to collaborative work and ways to overcome those obstacles.

- Learn team participant skills for the development of a document or presentation.

- Grasp team leader skills useful for steering a collaborative project to a successful conclusion.

"A camel is a horse designed by a team." "Too many cooks spoil the broth." Those two sayings communicate a common distrust about teamwork. Do you share that distrust, based on your experience with teams to date? This chapter shows, step-by-step, how to avoid the common pitfalls associated with the group development of a major document or presentation. A team has much to gain by mastering skills in collaborative work: Documents and oral presentations undertaken collaboratively are often more thoroughly researched, carefully designed, and efficiently written than similar projects taken on by a single writer. Moreover, such projects spring from a broader cross-section of the organization, which usually translates into greater buy-in from the company for the work product itself.

WHY TEAMS OFTEN HAVE TROUBLE WITH COLLABORATIVE PROJECTS

This chapter will investigate why many team members resist collaborative projects that involve developing a lengthy report, proposal, or presentation. Along the way we will discuss the importance, even the necessity, of the collaborative approach to many company communications. Then we will describe the step-by-step stages that teams can use in creating a major document or presentation. Finally, we will suggest practical techniques for team leaders who must supervise the collaborative efforts of their team members.

"It's easier to just do it myself." During your work or academic experience to date, you may have said these words about a team project that was hopelessly bogged down in disagreements, missed deadlines, and conflicting approaches. You may have had a team experience, for example, in which the eventual work product was supposed to be a report. Even though you related well to all other members of the team, complications in the project seemed to spring up from the very beginning. No one knew quite how to proceed or, just as bad, everyone had a different idea of how to get started and insisted their idea was the only good idea. When work finally got underway, some team members did too little and some did too much. Ill will crackled in the meeting room. Pieces of prose from individual team members didn't flow smoothly together to make a consistent document. Each team member wrote in a somewhat different style and could not be persuaded to write in any other manner. Finally, as in most cases of team collapse, one or two team members simply took charge of the project and did it themselves. Perhaps you were one of those brave souls. The team gave a collective sigh of relief to complete the project, but not one of the members found the collaborative process fulfilling or efficient.

Collaboration is a learned skill. Lacking that skill, team members may well find collaborative work inefficient and nettlesome.	**INSIGHT 58**

	Your Turn
Call to mind a group project or other collaborative attempt that did not go well. Analyze the causes for its failure.	

The frustrations and reservations you may have already experienced with the collaborative approach are usually due to one or more of the following factors:

Lack of Experience

Especially for new employees, the concept of developing a document or presentation as a team is quite new. Their experience through high school and college focused primarily on completing such work alone. Unauthorized assistance, in fact, was considered cheating. No wonder that many team members come to their first collaborative experience with little to offer and much to fear.

Lack of a Common Model

At the first team meeting with team members inexperienced in the collaborative approach to projects, it's not uncommon for each team member to describe, and even insist upon, his or her own way of developing a document or presentation. Listen in, for example, on these team voices:

Ralph: I think we all know approximately what we want to say. Let's just start on page one and write until we have a rough draft completed. That's the way I always did it in college. And I got good grades, by the way.

Manuel: That won't work, Ralph. Obviously the first thing we have to do is make an outline. All my teachers told me to begin with an outline, and that's what all the books say as well. Then we can divvy up parts of the outline and get this thing done.

Susan: How can we make an outline before we agree on our ideas, Manuel? Shouldn't we have a few meetings to agree on the basic ideas for our report before we even think about writing?

Linda: Wait a minute. A few meetings? We've got a deadline for this project and we can't just sit around talking. Let me try to write up the whole thing this weekend. Then you can all revise what I've done and put in any extra material you have. Don't worry, I'm a fast writer.

It's easy to see that such disagreements can quickly undermine the team's effort and eventual success. In such circumstances, the most senior or most powerful member of the team usually weighs in and has his or her way with the writing process. Grumbling, the rest of the team members give in and half-heartedly participate in the frustrating development process, but none does his or her best work. Some team members simply opt out of the process entirely or attempt to get reassigned.

Lack of Understanding About Relating to One Another

Inevitably in the process of team collaboration some team members will criticize and even discard the ideas or work samples of other group members. Unless the team knows how to work through such periods of disagreement, tempers will flare and work will grind to a halt. An important part of the collaborative process, therefore, involves successful group dynamics. On one hand, the team should not fall into GroupThink, described in Chapter 1 as the pressure to accept ideas solely to maintain group harmony. On the other hand, the team should not destroy itself by personal attacks, counterattacks, and hurt feelings. The team should seek a middle road where ideas and drafted work are evaluated fairly with a consensus view toward what's best for the emerging project.

INSIGHT 59	Simply knowing the main pitfalls to collaborative projects is the first step in avoiding those mistakes.

Your Turn

Think about a time when you were less than happy as a member of a collaborative team. Describe the source of your unhappiness. What eventually happened?

WHY COLLABORATIVE PROJECTS ARE GOOD FOR TEAMS AND GOOD FOR BUSINESS

The struggles of a team to work together on a collaborative project would matter less if business could get along without collaborate work—but it can't for at least five reasons.

First, participation in collaborative projects strengthens the work team itself. The value of collaborative writing, for example, lies not only in its end—a document completed on time—but in its means. Employees, often from different work units, join as team members and learn to work together toward a common goal. They experience the value of sharing expertise and accepting feedback. In short, they build the team spirit so crucial for corporate success.

Second, collaborative projects involve a political process. Few large corporations are pure dictatorships with the CEO barking out strict orders for employees to follow. Instead, many if not most companies organize according to what Douglas McGregor has called Theory Y principles (see Chapter 8), including participative decision making and shared work goals. In this kind of business, a manager doesn't put an engineer, a technical writer, a personnel officer, and a computer specialist on a collaborative team solely for the sake of their differing areas of expertise. The manager assembles this collaborative team to forge alliances and satisfy constituencies within the company. The engineering division, for example, may want to have its say in the document under development by the team; the inclusion of an engineer on the collaborative team assures that division that its interests will be represented.

Thus, when a collaborative team succeeds in working productively, different sectors around the company reap political dividends. Seeing this example of effective interaction on the team, divisions within the company become more cooperative and less likely to suspect the motives of other divisions. The collaborative team is the tip of an iceberg that extends deep into the political structure of the company.

A third reason business needs collaborative teams is that this approach to work reduces risk factors. Few companies can afford the risks involved in turning over a major document or presentation project to one individual. Even the most talented individual can be dead wrong at times. The company could face disaster if an incorrect or one-sided report goes forward from one individual without the checks and balances provided by other team members. Another risk is the dependence of a major project on the continued employment, health, or work habits of one individual. The team approach to collaborative development assures that the project will proceed, even if an individual on the team leaves the company or becomes ill.

Collaborative work incorporates more expertise—the fourth reason for its importance to business. No one person knows it all. Most important business documents and presentations discuss more than one point of view and come to a balanced conclusion. For those points to emerge, they must be represented on the team. Using the collaborative approach to document or presentation development, a safety specialist's expertise can temper a design expert's enthusiasm for a new product. A technical writer's skill can convey, in readable form, the precise data offered by a statistician.

The final reason collaboration is needed in business is that the process often makes the best use of company resources. When a contract is at stake or a government deadline looms, a company can't afford to have a solitary writer laboring for weeks on a project. The cost of assigning a team to develop a major project is justified if the result is winning the contract, meeting the deadline, or satisfying the client. Choosing a team for the project presumes, of course, that the team members know how to work together to get the job done. If they don't, one skilled writer-researcher might indeed do a better job than a disorganized, bickering team.

INSIGHT 60	Teams serve valuable functions for business far beyond their usefulness as a means of organizing work. Only effective teams, however, can fulfill those functions.

Your Turn	
Call to mind the last team of which you were a member. What purposes did it serve for the larger organization beyond its specific goals and deliverables?	

STEPS IN THE COLLABORATIVE PROCESS FOR DOCUMENTS AND PRESENTATIONS

The collaborative process follows these major steps:

- generate ideas
- organize information
- draft
- revise and edit

In the collaborative process, each of these important stages must be adapted to include the participation of the entire team. It won't do, in other words, to assign major parts of the development process to separate team members ("You think of the ideas. I'll do the writing") any more that two singers can divide a song into lyrics and melody. What follows, therefore, is a step-by-step plan for involving all team members in all stages of the development process for documents and presentations. These steps can be altered to suit varying business circumstances, as the needs of your purpose, audience, and resources dictate.

Step 1: Assemble a Team with Appropriate and Complementary Expertise

Too often, teams are formed on the basis of friendship, volunteers, or simply who's available. None of these approaches guarantees a group of writers with complementary skills and expertise. As a team leader in charge of assembling a collaborative team, consider both professional and personal qualities in deciding which team members will work best together.

The purpose of and audience for your project will determine what professional qualities various team members should bring to the team. For example, the writing of a flight training manual requires expertise from an experienced aviator, a training expert, an instructional writer, and probably a skilled illustrator. The writing of an annual report, by contrast, might well require one or more senior managers, a high-ranking financial officer, a professional writer, and others.

A variety of personality tests (including the well-known Myers-Briggs Type Indicator) can be used to determine the personality profiles of potential team members. Even if managers do not use such assessments, they can try to combine complementary types on the collaborative team. They might put a detail-oriented worker, for example, on the team to balance the influence of a bright but disorganized member. A writer with a lively, journalistic style might be brought aboard to keep a statistician from burying the project in numbers.

Step 2: Meet to Discuss What, When, Why, Where, How, How Much, and Who

What are we developing? In its first meeting, each member of the team must help answer this question. Let's say, for example, that a senior manager has assigned the team the task of writing a report on employee benefits. In this case, the team can decide the precise form of the document (in terms of length, organization, and format). From the beginning, all team members must reach agreement on the essential nature of the task: Is the report to be descriptive, giving details of past, present, and future employee benefit plans, or is the report also to be prescriptive, with recommendations for changing employee benefits in some way? Unless the team answers such initial questions, it cannot proceed productively to other stages in the development process.

When? Just as college assignments usually come with a deadline, so business tasks are tightly constrained by time. The development team must keep time limits in mind when making decisions about the topic range and research scope of the project. Length alone cannot be used to accurately determine how much time a project will take. Projects with short page counts, in fact, sometimes take much longer than more wordy documents. The French philosopher and mathematician Pascal captured this truth in a memorable line to a friend, albeit in French: "I'm sorry I haven't written a shorter letter, but I didn't have time."

Why? It isn't enough for senior management to have a reason for doing projects. Each member of the collaborative team must understand the business reasons and urgency for the project at hand. Team members who understand why they are writing a document, for example, have a much better chance of avoiding unnecessary digressions and blind alleys.

Where? The team must agree on the physical logistics of the collaborative process from the beginning. Where are team members physically located in the building? What communication links or useful software exists? Will the group meet in person or electronically, or both?

How? As we discussed earlier in the voices of Ralph, Manuel, Susan, and Linda, members come to the team with different approaches to the collaborative process. Therefore, they must discuss the process itself, with the goal of reaching a workable consensus. For example, all team members could review the steps set forth in this chapter or another book. Based on that review, the team could discuss and decide on the best way to accomplish the task before it.

How much? Money influences virtually every business decision. Collaboration, like all important business activities, costs the company money. (The salaries alone of four team members working for 1 week on a report could total $10,000 or more.) Instead of ignoring financial realities, the collaborative team should carefully assess how much the company wants to spend (in salaried time, research expenses, and support resources) to accomplish the project at hand. Operating within a budget may mean trimming the team's development plans for the project, but it's better to deal with financial limitations from the beginning rather than confront them later, when the project languishes overextended, half-finished, and underfunded.

Who? In this last agenda item of the first team meeting, the team designates a coordinator and perhaps other roles for team members. Sometimes, of course, the team coordinator is appointed in advance by senior management. If not, it's often better to wait until the end of an initial meeting to decide who will serve as leader or coordinator. In discussing the what, when, why, and other questions, the team has a chance to see each member in action. The team is then in a better position to choose as coordinator the member most likely to keep the team on track, on time, on budget, and not on each other's nerves.

INSIGHT 61	Thinking about the resource and time limitations placed upon a team's work is better undertaken at the beginning of the project than at a later stage.

Your Turn

For a team project on which you are now working or have worked recently, specify at least three resource limits and/or time constraints placed on your work. How did your team cope with these constraints?

Step 3: Meet in Person or Electronically to Generate Ideas

Most collaborative teams brainstorm their topics in face-to-face meetings. At these intense gatherings, team members try out ideas on one another. They listen, react, and avoid the temptation to settle on certain ideas too early in the process.

Especially when team members are separated by distance or scheduling conflicts, they can nevertheless generate ideas and bounce them off one another by means of the many groupware programs now available for collaborative work. The goal of idea generation is to produce not merely enough, but more than enough, useful ideas for the collaborative process. The team strives for as many and as far-reaching ideas as possible during the idea generation stage. Winnowing those ideas (selecting some, discarding others) comes later in the organization stage.

Step 4: Organize Ideas into a Working Outline

Some collaborative teams develop a working outline in a face-to-face meeting. Group members propose, challenge, argue, and compromise on each item in the growing outline until the full scheme lies before the team. Other teams choose to let each member form an organizational outline independently. Members then bring their outlines to a common meeting or share them electronically. In either case, the team reviews the various organizational approaches and puts together the best version—the working outline—from the many versions offered.

Step 5: Evaluate the Working Outline with the Help of Stakeholders

Before pursuing the hard work of research and writing that leads to the first draft of a document or presentation, the team takes time to evaluate the working outline with care. What does the boss or other significant audience member have to say about the outline? Does it satisfy the requirements and expectations of the company? Does the team have the talent, time, and resources to complete the project as outlined? Are all members of the team clear about the meaning of each item in the outline and the relations between those items (i.e., the logic of the outline)?

Step 6: Discuss and Undertake the Research Process

The team now investigates the full range of available research materials to elucidate and support the ideas and statements on the working outline. The coordinator of the team probably assigns portions of the outline to each team member for research. Members bring back their results to a common meeting or make them available to all members electronically.

Step 7: Discuss and Undertake the Drafting Process

Some collaborative teams operate by gradual accumulation. Individual members begin to draft small pieces of the project even during the research process. The team then decides which of those pieces fit well into the overall document and in what ways they should be expanded and connected.

Other collaborative teams require that each member turn over a carefully organized compilation of his or her research to one or two members who are responsible for actually drafting the document. In most cases, the drafters are the most proficient writers in the group—those with a special talent for style, clarity, and flow.

Rarely does a collaborative team compose each sentence of the first draft together. There are simply too many decisions to be made word-by-word in the drafting process for each team member to suggest and argue alternatives. Such discussion can be accomplished better at the revision stage.

The first draft, once completed, should be regarded by all team members as an exceedingly tentative document. In the understandable excitement of nearing the end of the project, too many collaborative teams consider the words of the first draft as text cast in granite. A better approach is to distribute the first draft electronically so that each team member can work through it to note his or her suggested changes.

INSIGHT 62   Few teams have success in beginning the drafting process too early in their collaborative work. Writing becomes quite difficult when you are unsure what you want to say.

Your Turn

Is it your habit to create an outline before drafting a document or presentation? How do you go about testing your outline to make sure it flows logically and makes your point? What use do you make of the outline in the drafting process?

Step 8: Evaluate the First Draft with the Help of Stakeholders

All team members now carefully review the completed first draft, looking for qualities of logic, persuasion, support, style, and format. There's no better occasion than this to see if the document suits its audience. If, for example, the project is being completed for senior management, the team may want to schedule a meeting to show these executives the first draft and talk through its major points. The team notes carefully all questions, criticisms, and comments from stakeholders as part of the agenda for the revision process.

Step 9: Revise the Draft for Consistency and Impact

No document is right until it is right for its audience. The team makes adjustments in logical flow, persuasive argumentation, level of diction, paragraph length, tone, format, illustrations, and all other aspects of the project with one goal in mind: to carry out the intended purpose of the document.

Step 10: Edit to Achieve Error-Free Text

Revision differs from editing in the way that farming differs from gardening. The team's revision efforts focus on larger matters of placement and style; those matters often require major renovation, reworking, or deletion. Editing, by contrast, takes a magnifying glass to each word, sentence, paragraph, footnote, and heading of the document. The team relies on iterative editing sessions by different pairs of eyes to catch every typo, misspelling, punctuation mistake, and other error.

These 10 steps describe a path, but not the only path, for the collaborative development of a document or presentation. If your team decides to skip one or more of the steps, take a moment to discuss what you're skipping and why.

Stakeholders, especially the primary audience to whom a document or presentation is addressed, should be involved as reviewers at early, middle, and late stages of the collaborative process.

INSIGHT 63

Your Turn

Bring to mind a collaborative project on which you worked. Specify the main stakeholders for that project. Tell how you involved them during the development process. If you did not involve them, tell why.

GUIDELINES FOR THE TEAM LEADER OF A COLLABORATIVE PROJECT

As team leader you have the challenging task of keeping the project moving forward with all members contributing to its development. Here are several distress signals from team members, with brief advice on how to deal with them:

"No one even listens to me." Your job as team leader is to make each team member feel valuable to the project and respected by team members. Inevitably, of course, some team members will contribute more than others, but the team leader should do everything possible (including personal conferences and assigned duties) to prevent malaise, withdrawal, or resentment from disrupting the work of the team.

"Who made you the boss?" Occasionally, a frustrated team member will directly challenge your role as team leader. In such cases, let others in the group speak for you, or you can remind the complaining team member that you have the support of other team members.

"What are we waiting for?" In any process involving the work of several people, occasional delays will occur as one team member waits for another to complete his or her work. Make sure that your team understands both the inevitability of glitches in the team process and the importance of completing work on which others depend.

"Where do you get off telling me I'm wrong?" We are all sensitive to negative criticism about the way we speak or write. That sensitivity carries over to the workplace, especially when one team member criticizes our work as "too wordy," "unclear," or "disorganized." We respond defensively—"Well, then, do it yourself!"—instead of understanding and possibly profiting from the interchange. As team leader, you should emphasize that criticism is directed at the work itself, not the person who wrote it. Conducting revision and editing sessions in a good-humored way goes far in alleviating the potential hostility that can develop when team members spar over language choices.

"I don't understand your changes." Especially as deadlines approach, the team leader and other members of the team may change the work of other members. If a team member requests an explanation, it's important for the team leader to provide one. Never simply say that a passage is "better my way." Doing so breeds ill will on the team and fails to teach the objecting team member preferable alternatives.

INSIGHT 64

Team leaders are inevitably the recipients, if not the targets, of complaints and frustrations from some team members. These leaders can help the team function harmoniously and efficiently if they strategize in advance on how to deal with the most common complaints and criticisms.

Your Turn

If you have led a collaborative effort of any kind, what types of complaints or criticism (if any) did you receive from team members? How did you respond to such comments? If you have not led a collaborative effort or received no complaints or criticism in your leadership role, what have been your main frustrations in serving on a collaborative team? What could the leader have done to address those problems?

Summing Up

Most teams are responsible for a deliverable of some kind, usually in the form of a report or presentation. Teams can be hobbled by the inexperience and resistance of their members in collaborating successfully on this kind of project. When team members and the team leader understand their roles in working together, the pitfalls of collaborative work can be avoided. Ten steps are recommended as a guide to the collaborative development of a document or presentation.

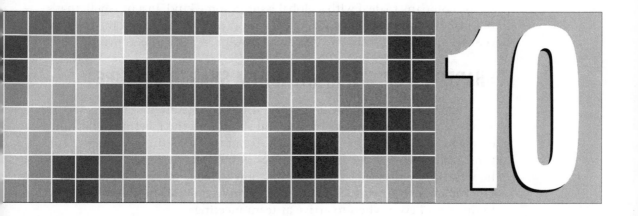

Developing Intercultural Teams

GOALS

- Recognize the increasing importance of intercultural and international teams in corporations and other organizations.

- Understand and adjust to the assumptions and practices of intercultural participants in teams.

- Make the most of the potential of intercultural teams to solve problems and seize opportunities.

Almost every major company you can name—Sears, Boeing, General Electric, IBM, and yes, McDonald's—has international branches that employ native workers. When these companies want to address a multinational problem or opportunity, they commonly assemble a team made up of members from their various branches throughout the world. Team members from India, Japan, France, Brazil, China, and the United States suddenly find themselves in a room—or in a teleconference—as members of an important team charged by the company to deal with a global issue of some kind. In a nutshell, that's the intercultural challenge facing more and more work teams in this new century—a challenge that may face you now or in your career future.

SHARED INFORMATION WITHOUT A SHARED CULTURE

Your team members on an intercultural team probably have access to the same company data that you do. As you sit around the meeting table, however, you soon realize that sharing data is not the same thing as sharing culture. Each person at the meeting brings quite different expectations about how and when to speak at the meeting, how to relate to the team leader and other members, when to socialize and when to talk business at meals, how to dress, and even when to arrive at team meetings.

These are all aspects of culture that we each carry with us, often unconsciously. Some things feel right and some things wrong, as judged by our cultural background. The goal of this chapter is not to ask you to set aside your own culture or become a devotee of another person's culture. Rather, the goal here is to become aware of the influence of various cultures on team processes. Once team members recognize the role of cultural difference operating within their team, they can deal constructively with those differences and often gain a competitive advantage because of them.

INSIGHT 65	Intercultural teams are a fact of business life. Their progress can be impeded if members are not skilled in making cultural adjustments.

Your Turn	
If you have worked abroad, briefly describe the cultural adjustments you had to make to function effectively in that region of the world. If you have not worked abroad, describe the cultural differences you have observed in a visitor or work associate new to this country. What did they do differently from American businesspeople? What behaviors would you advise them to change if they plan to work for a prolonged period in the United States?	

WHAT'S AT STAKE IN UNDERSTANDING CULTURAL DIFFERENCES

In earlier chapters we have seen how much the work of a team depends upon relationships forged among team members and with the team leader. In an intercultural team, the formation of these relationships depends, to a remarkable degree, on the willingness of all team members to

- be flexible and accepting of differences in values, beliefs, standards, and mores—even if they do not understand or personally believe in these differences
- be sensitive to verbal nuances and nonverbal behavior, as intercultural team members attempt to express their feelings as well as their thoughts
- be knowledgable about the religious, cultural, business, social, and dietary practices of other cultures
- be open in sharing aspects of your own culture at the same time you are learning about the cultures of your teammates

American team members sometimes have problems seeing beyond their own cultural assumptions in attempting to relate well with intercultural team members. By putting the spotlight on the following 10 assumptions, we can recognize them for what they are: American values and beliefs that may differ substantially from the perspectives of other, intercultural members of our team.

Assumption 1: Change Is Good

In the United States, change is often associated with progress, development, growth, and advancement. Many older world cultures do not share this basic belief. Instead, they view change as essentially disruptive and destructive. They value stability, preservation, tradition, and heritage.

Assumption 2: Time Controls Us

American businesspeople race against the clock and take time constraints seriously. Not to observe time commitments in the United States is a grave sign of disrespect or unprofessionalism. This is not so in much of the world. In many other cultures, business and other activities are not so rigidly controlled by time. "All in good time" is a common, relaxed attitude toward business projects in many cultures.

Assumption 3: We Are All Created Equal

Americans view equality as an important civic and social goal, but in most of the world, rank and status—often a part of one's birthright—are viewed as a natural part of everyday life and the source of one's authority. To many individuals in other cultures, personal progress out of their "class" is not a worthwhile goal. They have grown up knowing who they are and where they fit in the various strata of their society. Some, in fact, draw a sense of security from such knowledge.

Assumption 4: I Am an Individual with Special Interests and Needs, Including a Right to Privacy

Even though we are now a nation of more than 300 million people, each of us clings to some degree to the assumption of individualism, with attendant rights to be respected. In other cultures, where space is at a premium in homes, offices, and workplaces, and where large numbers of people are treated similarly, the American assumptions about individual rights and individual privacy are seen as merely quaint.

Assumption 5: We Are Self-Made People

In the United States we take cultural pride in making it on our own. We accept inherited wealth, but give the individual little personal credit for wealth secured from a parent. In other cultures, the self-made man or woman may not garner the respect accorded in the United States. "Old money" and old family or social connections may count much more for business influence than a person's track record of personal achievement.

Assumption 6: Competition Makes Us Feel Alive

Americans value competition and stress it as a desirable quality from the classroom to the sports field to the boardroom, but in societies that value cooperation, the intense competitiveness of the United States is not easy to comprehend. These societies place much more emphasis on the building of harmonious relationships among people, partnering with others to achieve common goals, and resisting the temptation to get ahead at the expense of others in the community or culture.

Assumption 7: The Future Looks Bright

People in the United States constantly work, plan, and strive for a better future. We set short- and long-term goals for our professional and financial lives. Much of the rest of the world, however, views an attempt to alter or improve the future as futile (and, in some cultures, even sinful). "What will be, will be" is a common attitude beyond our shores.

Assumption 8: Work Is the Only Game in Town

Americans work more hours per week than any other trading nation. Our work days and activities are scheduled weeks or even months in advance. We value work and the rewards of work so highly that many of us become workaholics. Many cultures do not share this obsessive attention to accomplishing productive labor; instead, they value a modicum of work balanced by a day strolling or meditating, frequent holidays with family and friends, and summer vacations much longer than their U.S. equivalents.

Assumption 9: We Tell It Like It Is

Americans are often viewed as being blunt to the point of rudeness. Our direct approach to people and situations may be difficult to understand for an individual who comes from a society where saving face is important or one in which an indirect method is used for conveying bad news or an uncomplimentary evaluation. Americans typically have little patience with people who hint at what they want to say rather than coming right out with it. From their vantage point, members of other cultures may have trouble trusting and respecting Americans who appear to have so little regard for the feelings of others.

Assumption 10: What Counts Is the Bottom Line

Americans are perceived around the world as being deeply materialistic. We talk about and care about our upscale appliances, cars, TVs, computers, and homes as our just rewards for hard work. Other cultures may view such materialism as spiritually shallow—the sad obsession of people who have not found deeper, less materialistic things to concern themselves with in life.

In this brief overview of some (but certainly not all) American assumptions and values, we have not attached labels of right or wrong to anyone's beliefs. Pointing out that much of the world does not share the American value system does not suggest that one group is correct and the other incorrect. Instead, we can use this knowledge of cultural difference to prepare ourselves for understanding and accepting intercultural team members on their own terms rather than assuming they are just like us.

Americans preparing for membership on an intercultural team can begin by examining their own assumptions and behaviors.	**INSIGHT 66**

Your Turn
Choose one aspect of American culture that you feel would not export well to another area of the world (of your choice). Explain why people in that area would have difficulty accepting the American cultural aspect you have chosen.

Team Manners for Intercultural Meetings

Most cultures are more formal than the United States in meeting behaviors, written documents, and oral presentations. Team members in the United States should be careful to use titles when addressing their team partners in Europe and Asia. It is almost always wise to use a surname and/or title when addressing a colleague in the work setting. A German professional may even be addressed as "Herr Dr. Professor" (three titles!).

In written communications with intercultural team members, opening sentences are usually introductory in nature rather than getting right to the point, in typical American fashion. Brief comments about a previous trip, the beauty of the locale, or other noncontroversial topic are quite appropriate as icebreakers for both written and spoken communications. Sensitive topics such as payments, behavior of company representatives, and errors or delays in shipping should be handled with deft timing, sensitivity, and tact.

In intercultural team conversations and meetings, American members should be careful to avoid terms that reflect superiority, power, or a lack of personal interest. This applies particularly to the giving and receiving of business cards from your intercultural associates. Throughout most of Asia, for example, it is expected that you will receive someone's business card with both hands, take a respectful moment to read it carefully and perhaps comment in a complimentary way on the person's title or company, then place the card in a special holder (rather than cramming it into an already over-stuffed wallet or purse). When giving your business card, you should extend it (again, with both hands) so that the print is readable from the perspective of the person receiving the card. This ritual almost always takes place upon first meeting your intercultural associate, not (as is often the case in American business practice) after a working relationship has been established.

Above all, take time to read about the cultural preferences, rituals, and habits of your intercultural associates before you meet them for the first time. You may even have the time and ability to master a few words in their native languages—a compliment to them, no matter how poorly you speak the words. Several good books on intercultural manners and mores are included in the Recommended Reading section at the end of this book.

INSIGHT 67	We tend to react in spite of ourselves to unusual verbal or nonverbal behaviors exhibited in meetings and other business occasions. Even though we understand that cultural differences explain these unusual behaviors, we often allow our attitudes and relationships to be shaped by our initial, judgmental reactions.

Tell about a time you were irritated or surprised by a verbal or nonverbal behavior on the part of a person new to U.S. culture. Did the person mean to offend you by the behavior? How can you avoid similar problems when you visit a culture that is new to you?

GRASPING THE DEEPER ASPECTS OF CULTURAL DIFFERENCE

If you intend to understand your intercultural team members in more than a surface way, you will inevitably have to come to terms with several profound cultural differences:

The perception of space. Animals, both wild and domestic, guard their territory. This concern for territoriality also exists in nations and cultures. To protect and define our territory we put up flags, fences, rows of bushes, signs, and so forth. The norms that govern our defense of territory are dictated by culture. Americans typically define an area of about 3 feet of open space around their personal territory (i.e., their bodies) as a comfort zone.

If you are a member of an intercultural team with participants from countries such as Mexico and Italy, you should expect them to intrude upon this culturally defined envelope of personal space. Your Italian member, for example, may be speaking with great excitement about a company development. As he does so, he moves to within a few inches of your face. You instinctively back up. Both of you experience an awkward and confusing intercultural moment. "Why is he moving so close to me?" you wonder. "Is he attacking me or is this a come-on of some kind?" Your Italian associate is just as confused. "Why is this person moving away from me? Am I saying something objectionable?"

Consider larger distributions of space from a cultural perspective. Look, for example, at the arrangement and division of space in a U.S. corporation. The president, in splendid isolation, occupies a large office on the top floor with corner windows. By contrast, French or Middle Eastern managing directors more commonly sit among their subordinates so they can observe all activities. Consider your Japanese associate who values a small, gem-like home characterized by elegant proportions and appointed with only the items needed for daily use. Contrast that attitude—and catch his looks of confusion—when he visits his first suburban American home measuring in the thousands of square feet and filled to the bursting point with possessions of all kinds.

INSIGHT 68	"Getting in my face" is considered a sign of hostility in the United States. It requires patience and practice to overcome these feelings when working on an intercultural team where social space is treated differently than in the United States.

Your Turn

Recall the last time that someone violated your personal space. Why did he or she do so? How did you react? What was the outcome of the situation?

The perception of time. Your intercultural team members may think of time quite differently than you do. In the United States, we save time, make time, spend time, waste time, and invest time. We distinguish between ordinary time and quality time. We become easily irritated when others do not observe time as obsessively as we do. Be prepared, therefore, for members of other cultures where punctuality is not a highly valued aspect of professional life; where "ripeness" of projects is more important than meeting deadlines; and where flexibility in scheduling and a casual attitude toward meeting times is the sign of a seasoned executive.

Friendships. As you get to know your intercultural team members over time, recognize that friendships are viewed differently from culture to culture. In the mobile U.S. society where people change jobs and locales frequently, we have all become accustomed to making new friends easily and quickly. New neighbors, church members, and work associates almost immediately become part of our social circle. When we attempt the same approach to friendship in other cultures—Germany, Japan, or Finland, for example—we may encounter a cultural surprise. Our acquaintances do not expect to become our friends. Friendships develop slowly and carefully in many cultures. In Welsh villages, for example, the "new couple" in town may have lived there 20 years or more—and still awaits full acceptance into the social life of the community. Be patient with intercultural team members, therefore, if they do not appear to warm up to you as quickly as you may have supposed they would. Instant friendship is often a new cultural experience for them.

Agreements. Perhaps most perplexing of all in working with intercultural team members is the question of "Do we have a deal or don't we?" To a U.S. businessperson, an agreement completed with a signed contract is almost sacred, but to many businesspeople in the Middle East, China, and elsewhere, a signed contract is just a piece of paper. More important by far in these cultures is the underlying relationship of trust established between parties over a series of meals. The signed contact, as many U.S. contractors have discovered to their dismay, is considered in many cultures to mark the beginning rather than the culmination of negotiation.

Ethical practices. These matters are among the most thorny for intercultural team members adjusting to one another's assumptions and business practices. What your intercultural team associate considers business as usual (including the giving of bribes or "commissions," as your team associate phrases it) may strike you as highly unethical. Certain comments or overt actions in a U.S. office between a man and woman may be termed sexual harrassment—actions that your intercultural team member views as harmless sport. It takes great skill to apprise your intercultural team members of the customary ethical codes and practices of your business environment without making them feel they are villains or worse. Difficult as it may be, this ethical education is crucial: You cannot afford to have a team representative acting on the basis of moral assumptions that are untenable and legally hazardous for your company.

INSIGHT 69

"When in Rome, do as the Romans do" is hardly an adequate guideline when basic matters of ethics and social justice are involved. When you confront assumptions or behaviors that offend your personal ethics or code of conduct, carefully review your options so that, if possible, you can achieve your business purpose without sacrificing your own integrity.

Your Turn

It is easy to think of the rest of the world as morally corrupt in contrast to a supposed law-and-order society here in the United States. Choose some part of the world, then put yourself in the shoes of a business visitor to the United States for the first time from that region. What aspects of American social or business life might that visitor find ethically or morally objectionable?

Male-female relationships. In interviews with intercultural teams, the topic that receives the most comment from team members is the matter of how men and women should relate in the workplace. Male-female relationships are a sensitive aspect of most cultures. If you visit a work associate in the Middle East, local custom dictates that you do not inquire about the health of his wife or daughters. Similarly off-limits are your inquiries into the whereabouts of wives as you are hosted by your male associates in Tokyo.

Americans have the most difficulty when they confront the spoken or unspoken assumption in intercultural team members that women are naturally subordinate to men in the order of things. The social, political, and moral dimensions of this issue come to a head when a U.S. businesswoman joins an intercultural team composed largely of members from cultures that suppress women. What is the woman to do? On the one hand, she could simply avoid contact with cultures who do not share her own culture's attitudes toward women. That option, however, may be professionally and economically hazardous for a woman's career. Although her specific choices will differ according to the culture and situation at hand, three trends have emerged in recent years:

1. Businesswomen are visiting sexually hostile cultures in increasing numbers. The American businesswoman in a Middle Eastern business meeting is no longer seen as an oddity.
2. When businesswomen anticipate problems due to sexual assumptions, they prepare in advance by establishing their professional status with their foreign clients through correspondence, telephone conversation, and mutual acquaintances. When they arrive in the foreign culture, these early contacts help these women arrive as "people" rather than as women.
3. Women sometimes make initial business contacts in the company of male associates, who then withdraw as the business relationship develops.

Attitudes toward women in business are quickly changing around the world as women assert themselves as professionals no less qualified than men to do business. It remains sad, however, when American-born Japanese businesswomen who speak fluent Japanese purposely speak only English when they visit Japan on business so that they will not be treated like a Japanese woman (i.e., given little professional respect).

INSIGHT 70	Women face an ongoing struggle throughout much of the world to be accepted on a par with men for business purposes. When women confront suppression and prejudice, they can strategize to overcome these factors.

Your Turn

If you are a woman, describe a time when you were devalued as a professional because of your gender. What did you do about the situation? If you are a man, describe a time when you observed a woman placed or kept in a subordinate role primarily because of her gender. What did you do about the situation?

COMMUNICATION IN THE INTERCULTURAL TEAM MEETING

People take for granted that verbal language differs from culture to culture, but your team members may be less aware that nonverbal language also varies dramatically across cultures. Mixed signals due to a misreading of nonverbal cues has proven a barrier in many intercultural team meetings.

Nonverbal signs and cues can range from touching and sniffing to gestures and body movement. The attitude in the United States toward the nonverbal area of touching another work associate is vastly different from that of many other cultures. It is not unusual throughout Europe and the Middle East to see two men walking arm in arm or with an arm encircling a shoulder. At a meeting, a work associate in these countries may place a hand on the forearm of the person sitting nearby and keep that hand there while talking.

Expected business posture also differs substantially from culture to culture. Discussion in a team meeting in the United States might find members in very relaxed postures. A man may even have a foot propped on a nearby chair or planted on a tabletop. Not so in Korea, the Middle East, China, Japan, and much of Europe. There, sitting "at attention" is a sign of respect to your team leader and fellow members. Showing the soles of your feet to your Saudi associates would be an insult indeed. Keeping your hands in your pockets while addressing your German or Austrian boss would be a sign of disrespect.

Perhaps most difficult to adjust to are cultural differences having to do with eye contact. In the United States we show concern when the other person does not look us in the eye or seems otherwise evasive. Is there a lack of honesty or integrity here, we wonder? But in Japan, a business leader may infer a lack of respect if a subordinate does give direct eye contact. When serving on an intercultural team, do not impute U.S. conclusions to eye contact behaviors exhibited by members of other cultures. This particular nonverbal difference is the first to be noticed and remains the hardest to change for intercultural team members attempting to adjust to U.S. ways.

INSIGHT 71

Among the most difficult intercultural differences to adjust to are touching, posture, and eye contact behaviors. We tend to have knee-jerk reactions to what we perceive as abnormal behaviors in these categories. We may experience difficulty in preventing these reactions from interfering with our relationships with intercultural team members.

Your Turn

Tell about a time when you noticed an unusual nonverbal behavior on the part of a visitor new to this country. How did you react? Why?

Summing Up

Intercultural teams are an increasing reality for U.S. businesspeople. The success of the team will depend in large part upon the willingness of team members to adjust to the many cultural differences they observe in one another. Learning to see a colleague as different but not "less than" is the key to productive team relationships. Members come to understand that they can respect and live with cultural differences in others even when they do not accept those values, practices, or worldviews for themselves.

Recommended Reading

Blanchard, Ken et al. *High Five! The Magic of Working Together.* New York: William Morrow & Co., 2000.

Demarco, Tom et al. *Peopleware: Productive Projects and Teams.* New York: Dorset House, 1999.

Fisher, Kimball. *Leading Self-Directed Work Teams.* New York: McGraw-Hill Professional Publishing, 1999.

Katzenbach, Jon R. et al. *The Wisdom of Teams: Creating the High-Performance Organization.* New York: Harperbusiness, 1994.

Kelsey, Dee et al. *Great Meetings! How to Facilitate Like a Pro.* New York: Hanson Park Press, 1999.

Kinlaw, Dennis C. *Superior Teams: What They Are and How to Develop Them.* New York: Gower Publishing, 1998.

LaFasto, Frank M. et al. *When Teams Work Best: 6,000 Team Members and Leaders Tell What It Takes to Succeed.* New York: Sage Publications, 2001.

Maxwell, John C. *The 17 Indisputable Laws of Teamwork: Embrace Them and Empower Your Team.* New York: Thomas Nelson, 2001.

Niemela, Cynder. *Leading High Impact Teams: The Coach Approach to Peak Performance.* New York: High Impact Publishing, 2001.

Putz, Gregory B. *Facilitation Skills: Helping Groups Make Decisions.* New York: Deep Space Technology Co., 1998.

Roming, Dennis A. *Side by Side Leadership: Achieving Outstanding Results Together.* New York: Bard Press, 2001.

Wellins, Richard S. *Empowered Teams: Creating Self-Directed Work Groups That Improve Quality, Productivity, and Participation.* San Francisco: Jossey-Bass Management, 1993.

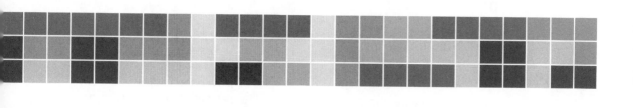

Index